Contents

Anthony Skuse is a director, dramaturg and teacher. His directing credits include: Simon Stephen's *On the shore of the wide world* (Griffin Independent); Amy Hertzog's *4000 Miles* (Under the Wharf, Sydney & La Boite Brisbane); Simon Stephen's *Punk Rock* (Under the Wharf), which received three Sydney Theatre Awards for Best Independent Production, Best Direction and Best Actor in a Supporting Role; Henry Purcell's *Dioclesian* (Pinchgut Opera); Tracy Letts' *Bug* (Picture This and Griffin Independent); Jose Rivera's *References to Salvador Dali Make Me Hot* (Artsradar and Griffin Independent); Marius Von Mayenburg's *The Cold Child* (2006 Griffin Stablemates); Michael Gow's *Live Acts On Stage* (square the circle and 2005 Griffin Stablemates); Robert Faquar's *Bad Jazz* (square the circle and Darlinghurst Theatre); Mark Ravenhill's *pool (no water)* (square the circle and Darlinghurst Theatre); The Presnyakov Brothers' *Terrorism* (Darlinghurst Theatre Sydney); Janis Balodis' *Too Young For Ghosts* (NIDA); Tony Kushner's *Bright Room Called Day* (NIDA); *The Greek Project: Aischylos, Euripides and Sophocles*: a special project at ATYP, for twenty women, aged nine to sixty-nine. Anthony teaches at Actors Centre Australia, as well as at Sydney's College of Fine Arts and NIDA, where he taught Repertoire with Playwrights from 2009 to 2012. Training: Drama Studio Sydney.

THE VOICES PROJECT 2014:
BITE ME

Pip Nat Georgie by Jory Anast
Tell Me by Jake Brian
Sweet Sour by Sophie Hardcastle
Sweet in the Savoury by Tasnim Hossain
Something I Prepared Earlier by Julian Larnach
Dig In Dean by Zac Linford
Facon by Felicity Pickering
Eating Sunshine by Emily Sheehan
That Daniel by Joel Tan
Food, Baby by Kyle Walmsley
George by Keir Wilkins

The Language of Love by Kim Ho
Hunger by Brooke Robinson

CURRENCY PRESS
SYDNEY

ATYP
Australian Theatre
for Young People

CURRENCY PLAYS

First published in 2014
by Currency Press Pty Ltd
PO Box 2287 Strawberry Hills NSW 2012
enquiries@currency.com.au
www.currency.com.au

National Library of Australia CIP data

Title:	The voices project 2014 : bite me / Jory Anast [and twelve others].
ISBN:	9781925005073 (paperback)
Series:	Voices project
Target audience:	For young adults
Subjects:	Monologues.
	Australian drama.
Other Authors/Contributors:	
	Anast, Jory, author.
Dewey Number:	808.8245

Cover design by Holly Fraser. Photographer: Zan Wimberley.

This publication was supported by the Copyright
Agency Limited Cultural Fund and the Graeme
Wood Foundation

Currency Press acknowledges the Traditional Owners of the Country on which we live and
work. We pay our respects to all Aboriginal and Torres Strait Islander Elders, past and present.

Introduction
Anthony Skuse

In July I drove down to the writer's retreat at Bundanon to hear eighteen new monologues read by the Fresh Ink 2013 writers. We sat in a circle on the verandah overlooking the Shoalhaven River as the sun set and the mosquitoes came out. It was quite extraordinary. I realised that working with new writing is a delicate business. Exciting but delicate. Exciting because as night fell and the bodies receded, it was the voice and the language that drew me into these narratives. Delicate in the way these stories hung in the air, each one fired by a different sense of longing. Exciting because these are young voices speaking to and about their experience of living in all its complexity.

I was surprised by the diversity of their responses to the overarching theme of food. The preparing and eating of food, as well as the thing itself, becomes the metaphor for belonging and loss, for love and sadness.

Oddly perhaps the project's title BITE ME reminds me of Lewis Carroll's Alice, and the little bottle with the paper label tired round its neck, and the words DRINK ME beautifully printed in large letters. In Wonderland food is an agent for change and transformation. Later when she comes across a second bottle she ruminates 'I know something interesting is sure to happen whenever I eat or drink anything.' And so it is with this collection of monologues,* one bite and they will crash around your mouth and roll along your taste buds. Delicious!

---

* This collection also includes the monologue *The Language of Love* by Kim Ho, which was turned into a phenomenally successful online film by director Laura Scrivano, and *Hunger* by Brooke Robinson from *The Voices Project 2012: The One Sure Thing*, which also was made into a film for The Voices Project, under the direction of Stephen McCallum.

JANE BODIE is a playwright, screenwriter, mentor and director. Jane's plays include *Music* (Griffin 2014); *This Years Ashes* (Griffin 2011); *Us* (Hampstead Theatre UK); *Hallelujah* (Theatre 503 UK); *Out Of Me* (Soho Theatre UK); *Ride* (Belvoir Company B, 59E59 New York); *A Single Act*, winner of The Victorian Premiers Literary Award 2007 (MTC/Hampstead Theatre UK); *Still, Hilt* and *Fourplay* (Trades Hall, TRS and Edinburgh Fringe). Jane was short listed for The Ewa Czajor Memorial Award for her work as a director. She was nominated for the Patrick White Playwrights' Award and won a Green Room Award for Outstanding Writing in 2003 for *Still*. Jane worked at the Royal Court Theatre with the Young Writers Programme and was one of the writers chosen for an attachment at the National Theatre in the UK in 2005. Jane has also written extensively for TV and radio, including several plays for Radio National and Radio 4 in the UK. Her writing for TV includes *The Secret Life of Us, Tashi, Crash/Burn, No Angels* and *Moving Wallpaper*. She is currently working on a screenplay for Channel 4/Altered Image in the UK and adapting her play *This Years Ashes* for the screen for Screen Australia. Jane also works as a playwright teacher and dramaturg. She was Head of Playwriting at NIDA from 2010–2012 and is currently Associate Artist at the Griffin Theatre, as well as working with Playwriting Australia as a mentor and dramaturg. Jane led the Sydney cohort of the 2013 4x4 Fresh Ink mentoring program, and was a tutor at the 2013 Fresh Ink National Studio, where the BITE ME monologues were developed.

ABOUT FOOD
Jane Bodie

In order to write about food, I have to admit something very shameful.

I recently read an article in *Who Weekly* (and that's not even the shameful thing) and the reading of this article led to me buying a cookbook by Gwyneth Paltrow. And I hate Gwyneth Paltrow. I hate the name of her website, *GLOOP*, I hate her husband's band, I even hate the name of her children, Apple, and Tapioca. But, the thing is, I really don't hate food.

The article was about a health collapse Ms Paltrow had due to her transatlantic hectic schedule and the occasional glass or red, or a slice of toast late at night, how very dare she. This, so the article claimed had caused her to have a meltdown, her hormones and adrenals were out of whack, causing a total collapse of her immune system. In fact, Ms Paltrow thought she was dying. The only solution, so her guru like Doctor proclaimed, was to give up wheat, sugar, dairy, shellfish, meat, wine, coffee. All the good stuff, in fact the very stuff that makes life worth living. She did this, no doubt with the help of an entourage of mini personal chefs and shoppers, and felt, like a new woman. The result, a cook book of dishes made from the only food allowed, and a cavalier suggestion we should all give this crazy diet a try and see how easy it is. The recipes seemed to involve a lot of quinoa, kale and mist. But the book—if you can ignore the smug photos of her in sun hat with baskets laden with organic purple carrots—is actually surprisingly good. I've even discovered I love kale.

I should say at this point, I'm not averse to eating my greens, or healthy eating at all. I've suffered from food allergies all my life, which is my excuse for buying the book. However, I do object to the recent-ish fad of the demonising of certain foods, and the fact this seems to be making us paranoid, suspicious and full of fear, rather than, well, happier, healthier. Somewhere along the line, the idea of food as nourishment, joy, celebration, seems to have been lost. And this got me thinking about my father, as most things do.

Because when I told my dad my eczema was a result of my allergy to wheat, his response—as a man who always finished every meal by mopping his plate bone dry with two slices of sliced bread—was 'Wheat, you're allergic to wheat, as in bread—don't be ridiculous Jane.' (My father wasn't much of a chef—once when I was staying at his house and sick with food poisoning, he brought me a bowl of soup from a tin to my room—when I sipped a little and felt better, he seemed pleased with himself. Later that day he returned to my room with a bowl of Lobster Bisque, also from a tin. I sat up, smelt it and promptly vomited.)

But my dad made brilliant breakfasts, perfect unequalled golden moist scrambled eggs, bacon, just the right level of crisp and mushrooms to die for, all served with hard-core plunger coffee, that you could stand a spoon up in. Waking to breakfast at his house, was like being in a normal family, for a moment. Sitting down at the table, half asleep and smelling like a teenager and being handed a plate of this perfect meal by him, in his dressing gown, was like being loved, in the right way. So when years later my father died from a brain tumour, it's only fitting that after a period of four months of violent grieving (when I refused to get out of bed, wash, certainly not to cook, or eat), it took a cunning plan of my friends, to get me out and back into life.

It was August, five months exactly after my fathers death and my birthday loomed, which I had no plans of celebrating. My friends suggested I throw a party, at my new flat, that had barely seen the light of day, since dad had gone. They said they could do the food for it, I'd just have to get up, vacuum and probably shower, possibly even brush my hair. I hadn't the energy to refuse, and Leo girl that I am, something about the gauntlet being thrown down, of them cooking food for my party, *my* party, managed to irritate me out of bed and into the shower.

We had a week. Friends divvied up dishes they'd bring, organised cheese and cracker rostas and planned cakes (I'm not a cake maker, it's all far too precise). I agreed to cook the four main courses; fish pie, roast Lamb, Chicken tandoori and, my dad's favourite, potato salad. I shopped slowly, like a ghost, and then two days before the party,

I began to cook. I'm not sure how I began, but somehow I woke up, and slowly began to peel things. I boiled and roasted things in their skins, tasted ingredients, I found serving plates and opened wine, I played music for the first time in months. I opened up the blinds, the windows, and let light and the day in. I cooked for two days, as people dropped off wine, dishes and extra cutlery. My ex-boyfriend weeded my garden and built a BBQ out of bricks and an old fireplace my dad had brought round and dumped in my garden, with no explanation. At last, a use for it.

The party was a huge success. It was a feast, a celebration. Everyone I've ever loved (well, except for my dad) came. There was so much food, that people stayed and ate and slept, and fell in love and talked to old friends and made new friends and slept over and woke and washed up and ate again. And standing in my garden, watching my friend Claire, who is a vegan, tucking into a steaming plate of my fish pie, on that gloriously dappled August afternoon in my own garden, stuffed with food and surrounded by people, happy, sated, joyful, full of flavour, the smell of barbequing tandoori in the air, I realised that life would and could go on. That there would always be days like this. And I felt full.

Because food is life.

The way people feel about food, the way they think and relate to it, the food they love and hate, how it makes them feel, act, communicate, how they cook for themselves or the people they care about, says so much about who they are, at their very core. It says everything about how they see and act in the world, how they give, and take, how they choose to live. As a writer, thinking about food makes me think of so many important things, maybe all the important things—love, joy, sex, my childhood, growing up, friendships, sharing, family, dates, parties, wine, hangovers, breakfasts, midnight snacks, holidays, winter nights, summer mornings, the earth, the sky, home, caring for people, my body, guilt, health, sickness. Death. So what could be better than the opportunity to write a piece of theatre about food? To give words to all that food is and can be about, like being able to create an entirely new flavour with words. Not much could be better than that.

So in closing, I suppose what I want to say is that I love food about as much as I love writing. Which is a lot. Spending time at Bundanon with the Fresh Ink writers, getting to know them and talk about food and then eat together for a week, and then hearing their monologues on food was, well, delicious. So may you savour these monologues, time and time again, and with as much love, courage, variety of experience and an appreciation of the fine ingredients that I know went into writing them.

Fresh Ink Writers Studio at Bundanon (photo Dan Prichard)

Kim Ho was born and raised in Sydney. Throughout his schooling, he was heavily involved in music and drama, performing in plays such as *The Popular Mechanicals*, Louis Nowra's *Cosi* and Monty Python's *Spamalot*. He is also involved in community theatre, and has played an ungodly number of animals: springboks, foxes, crabs and horses. And a tumbleweed. Kim enjoys storytelling in all its forms, and has made several short films for Tropfest Jr. However, he really began focusing on dramatic writing in 2012. The success of *Transcendence* in The Voices Project's Love Bytes competition led to a mentorship with Tommy Murphy. Together, they developed his monologue *The Language of Love*, which enjoyed worldwide exposure. In 2013, he was a recipient of the Besen Family Artist Programme, Writer's Development at Malthouse Theatre. Kim is currently developing a deliciously wicked black comedy, and devours every play he finds.

THE YEAR OF LOVE
Kim Ho

As its title suggests, *The Language of Love* is a monologue about the hazards and joys of communication. It's a coming out story, sure, but it's also about the courage to speak. As a young writer and performer, I am particularly aware that self-expression requires you to be brave and articulate. The monologue is essentially my attempt to understand how we can fly in the face of logic and find the strength to speak our minds.

It's perhaps ironic, then, that it all started life in Maths class. While my friends grappled with calculus, I was scribbling furiously at the back of the class. The goal: to submit something for The Voices Project's competition, Love Bytes. The brief: write, film and upload a three-minute monologue about love. The catch: I knew very little about monologues, and even less about love. But, driven by a potent mix of naïvety and curiosity, my little piece, *Transcendence*, was taking shape. The original inspiration was a short advertisement for GetUp Australia called *It's Time;* the message of equal love struck me as a very important and urgent moral issue. [***Editor's Note:*** *It's Time* was directed by Stephen McCallum, who also directed Brooke Robinson's *Hunger* for The Voices Project. Read an interview with Stephen about *Hunger* on page 19.] Just hours before the deadline, I hastily filmed and edited it together—a misshapen but optimistic take on a boy admitting he has feelings for his best friend.

To my great surprise, the judges enjoyed my writing and Dan Prichard, Fresh Ink Manager and producer of The Voices Project, approached me with the idea of a mentorship with playwright Tommy Murphy. All I had to do, he said, was develop it into a longer work for filming.

Simple as that, right?

Nope: I battled hard, at first. My initial instinct was to try and use my monologue as an indictment of religious-based homophobia, but I couldn't find the human message inside that premise. The breakthrough came when reading Tommy's work. There was warmth in his writing that was immediately apparent and I devoured three plays in quick succession, crying and chortling my way through. Tommy treats his characters with a remarkable compassion and respect. Taking me on numerous strolls around Surry Hills, he urged me to think of dramatic writing as an exercise in empathy. Theatre exists to entertain, I learned; it's not a vehicle to lecture the audience on your own point of view. Start with a character, and let your story grow from there.

And so Charlie began to take shape, with his own dreams, faults, quirks and, crucially, secrets. I wanted to make his story relatable to a diverse audience, so it's less concerned with coming out than conquering fear—of exams, of expressing your feelings for someone, of losing your most trusted ally, of not knowing who you really are, and of facing the ridicule of a society that doesn't yet accept you. The monologue's assertion that all love is equal rested on Charlie's 'relatability,' so I wanted my audience to get to know him a bit before they discover his sexuality. He's a person, not an issue, and I treated him as such.

In tandem with writing, I was doing a substantial amount of research. I watched some teenagers' coming out videos on YouTube and stood in awe of their bravery. One boy in particular showed an emotional maturity beyond his age: 'Some people will be hating me... please don't post it. Why are you watching this video if you hate it?' To my dismay, I learnt that this boy had been forced to take down his channel due to the amount of vitriol directed at him.

He was only twelve years old.

More and more, I knew that the film had the potential to do a lot of good, but I felt a responsibility to write something that remained respectful to the LGBTI community. Most importantly, I wanted to write something that would resonate with people regardless of their sexuality.

Tommy helped me through six drafts before handing me over to our director, Laura Scrivano. We agreed that performing my own writing would be a challenge, but might make the piece seem that bit more authentic. Laura is a performance-based director, and her process helped breathe life into the text. We found new rhythm and nuance I hadn't been conscious of as a writer, fresh ways of looking at familiar phrases.

Towards the end of January, performer, director and crew converged to shoot the film, now called *The Language of Love,* with a greater focus on French as a metaphor for self-expression. Tommy, Laura, Dan and I agreed unanimously on setting the film in an examination hall, agreeing that we could emphasise solitude by placing Charlie amidst a sea of empty desks. Tragically, when he needs help the most, he's alone... except for the viewers. I persuaded some friends to voluntarily sit an exam with me in a big old hall at Sydney Grammar School, and after eleven hours on set we wrapped, exhausted but content.

The film was cut together over the next two months, and released online in early April, 2013. We were lucky enough to have Sydney's MP Alex Greenwich attend the première at the Australian Film, Television and Radio School: a small but enthusiastic gathering of cast, crew and friends. But as the view count across YouTube and Vimeo grew, we realised that the film was exceeding our wildest expectations.

Stephen Fry was first. Tweeting the film resulted in so much traffic he crashed Fresh Ink's website. ArtsHub and the *Sydney Morning Herald* increased that exposure. Clover Moore and Danii Minogue joined in the support on Twitter. I got to speak on national radio in Australia and America. The film was mentioned in the Herald (again), leading US gay publication the *Advocate*, the *Huffington Post*, *Buzzfeed* and *Upworthy*. It screened at the Tasmania Queer Film Festival (before *The Rocky Horror Picture Show*!) and the Shanghai Pride Festival, and was short listed for Cardiff's Iris Prize. We'd almost finished hyperventilating when Ellen DeGeneres tweeted the film, giving us 90,000 views in a day. I cannot begin to explain how proud (and completely surprised) the whole team feels when we look back at this journey.

Most important for us, though, was the extent to which *The Language of Love* connected with people all around the world, particularly LGBTI youth. The amount of positive feedback floored us—viewers of all ages and sexual orientations commented that the film's message of love, friendship and hope deeply moved them. In our own small way, we seem to have challenged heteronormativity and homophobia and started conversations about traditional perceptions of love. I hope that our little film—made on a tiny budget with a few, passionate people—will continue to share ideas of tolerance, acceptance and courage in the face of adversity.

In fact, above all else, this process has taught me the importance of courage and having a go. Despite the monologue's ambiguous ending, Charlie 'wins' because he confronts his fears. In a similar way, if I'd been too paralysed by my own inexperience to write *Transcendence*, I would have missed out on some monumentally groovy opportunities. Being a young artist affords a special type of impunity. Exploit it for all it's worth! Write, act, film. Make mistakes and learn. More than anything, the artistic community rewards courage.

So be brave. Take the plunge.

[*Editor's Note:* Find out more about the making of the film and its online journey, and watch *The Language of Love* at www. thelanguageoflovefilm.com]

Kim Ho in atyp's filmed monologue *The Language of Love* (photos Ross Giardina)

Stephen McCallum is one of Australia's leading shorts and music video director. In 2012 his short film about gay marriage, *It's Time*, was seen by more than 12,000,000 people worldwide. He directed *Hunger* for The Voices Project, from Brooke Robinson's monologue for *The Voices Project 2012: The One Sure Thing*.

INTERVIEW WITH STEPHEN McCALLUM

How did you get involved in The Voices Project?

I first came onto *The Voices Project* through my friend Laura Scrivano (director of *The Language of Love*, *Boot: The Original Monologue* and *Little Love)*, who suggested I meet with Dan Prichard at **atyp**, the producer of The Voices Project, to talk about the program. I'd really liked Laura's films from the previous year and I thought it was a really interesting way to present a monologue, especially *Little Love*. I could see myself doing something like that and taking it into a slightly different direction, a more visual direction. I saw them as more of an art installation, a more surreal moodpiece—I thought there was a real opportunity to create something visually striking. So I met with Dan and I was given the 21 existing monologues and I got to choose and the one I chose was *Hunger*.

That first meeting was really interesting because I like having restrictions when I'm filming and I was told: You've got one day to shoot it, one actor, you can't change any of the dialogue and it's a seven-minute monologue. I was like: GREAT! That's good as that presents immediately a number of challenges after choosing the monologue, the main one being: how **do** you make one actor, talking to a camera, interesting for seven to ten minutes?

Why did you go for Hunger*?*

For me, *Hunger* was a standout because it immediately had visuals. It's written in such a strange way and was very different from the others because it was percussive—I'm from a musical background and you could almost see edit points in the lines, and images would flash forward. Because of that, it's very evocative and so that's very attractive to me. I always try to think of things visually and how to create an emotional response with visuals. My initial instinct was to make it in quite a surreal, nightmarish manner, which is what I thought was already initially on the page so then it was just a question of meeting with Brooke (Robinson, the writer) and seeing if I was the right fit for how I was thinking about it. I wanted to use *a lot* of imagery to put across the emotional subtext of the character, and my idea was to use projections.

Brooke was very cool and just said 'Cool! Go for it.' She gave me complete freedom to do that and seemed excited about that direction as well, which was very cool as a lot of times as a filmmaker you don't get to have that much freedom so it was really good to just run with it. I did it with my crew as well and that's been the process all the way along, to be very instinctive. It has to feel right but it also had to honour the feeling in the script.

How did you work with Tom Stokes, who plays Sam?

It was really challenging for Tom to get his head around who the character is talking to because it's quite a schizophrenic script—at one point Sam is talking as himself, at another impersonating another person and then also being an almost omniscient force in certain aspects. He really had to jump back and forth so he did really well. We also identified that Sam is talking to the head chef but we imagined the head chef in different modes—so at one point the head chef is right over him, then at another he's tied up.

And how did you visualise the film?

I really connected with the dreamlike nature of the piece. The monologue is either incredibly confronting and intense and abrasive, or it's very dreamy and peaceful and I was very interested in that light and shade, that tension and release, which we tried to bring out in the filming.

So when I first read the script, I had lots of imagery coming to me. Sam's talking about the kitchen, and I imagined sparks and fire and I was asking myself how I could make that visually happen? After a couple of workshops with Tom, I came up with the idea of using projections behind the actor but whatever I did visually, I didn't want to get in the way of his performance. I didn't want Tom to be aware of it at all, so having the projections behind him, he could get on with the performance and move through the different modes of his performance without being affected any more than is usual with cameras and lights and sound people!

One of the first things I had to grapple with is that the play is set in a kitchen, but it's not a real kitchen—for me it's like this dreamscape, this nightmarish world and a kind of heavenly world as well that he goes into. So I thought that if you put it in an actual physical kitchen, it's going to ruin that atmosphere, so I figured that there was enough description in the dialogue that the imagery of the kitchen will come across anyway. It was more about capturing the subliminal feeling of that kitchen.

So how was the shoot?

It was pretty guerilla filmmaking. We had enough budget but, how I wanted to film it was quite challenging. We shot in a warehouse in Marrickville (Sydney) over a day, and we had a projection screen behind the actor. We shot it pretty much chronologically and we had to break every three minutes for Boeing 747s flying over the Marrickville flight path. We really didn't know that was going to be such a problem—every time we scouted the location, it was really quiet but as we were filming at the weekend, there were ten times as many planes…

Beyond that, because the monologue is quite lengthy and quite exhausting for an actor, and because there's a lot of different moods, each part of the monologue has its own specific look. We split it down to specific two-minute chunks. So each part of the monologue, depending on the mood of the character, has its own specific look, attempting to solve the problem of keeping the monologue visually interesting and stimulating for the seven to ten minutes.

The sound track is really unusual. Can you tell us how that was developed?

The design of the sound and music was very interesting because my sound designer was in Perth and my composer, Damien Lane, is based in Sydney. So we've been working via DropBox essentially, sending files back and forth, but you've got to make sure the composition of the music doesn't step on the toes of the sound design, and vice versa so those guys have been communicating. For me, I like them to blend together—I don't want them to appear separate. At certain points, I've told them not to communicate with each other because I want it to clash.

So looking back on the film, how was the whole experience?

I've really enjoyed the whole thing, because I've really enjoyed the freedom to trust my instincts to just go with it. I always find that when you do that you get the best results, and when you communicate that to your crew you get the best out of them. It starts with the script, and Brooke's script had all that in it, so it was just a matter of honouring that and everyone coming on board with the vision to bring it to life.

The film takes me into a different type of world and I hope the audience feels the same as I do and that each part of the film— performance, editing, music—is part of that world.

Watch *Hunger* at www.youtube.com/TheVoicesProject

Top: *Hunger* director Stephen McCallum, star Tom Stokes. Bottom: *Hunger* director Stephen McCallum, writer Brooke Robinson and star Tom Stokes (photos Tim Barnsley)

Pip Nat Georgie

Jory Anast

We played shoot, shag or marry the other day. Down at Musgrave Park. Your name came up. It was between you, Nat and Pip. I didn't know what to pick, so I backed out of the game and the fellas called me a little bitch, so thanks for that. My first instinct was to marry you, shag Natalie and shoot Pip, because you're my best mate and I guess if I had to marry someone at least you and I would have a fun time, but then I remembered that Nat has chlamydia and Pip's actually pretty nice—probably because she's so ugly, but I suppose ugliness isn't a really good enough reason to die, so I rearranged it. I tried marrying Pip, shooting Nat and shagging you, but I don't think I could cope with sleeping with you just the once because even though your tits are fucking phenomenal I don't think it would be worth what it would do to our friendship. I mean it would definitely be worth it but maybe not in the long run, plus Garret would bash the shit out of me and even though I reckon in a fair fight I could take him, Garret's never really fought that fair. Cos he's a dick. No offense. And even my own safety aside, I remember that time in grade 11 when Lachlan banged you and bounced out, and how much it affected you.

I know at the time I was a bit of a dick about it, and I remember you slapped me for that. I was glad you did though, that your sadness had moved off of you and turned into anger towards me, because the truth is I hated the look on your face when you told me what he did to you, when you said you felt that he took a piece of you—I pictured that you were an island and he was smuggling conch shells off of your shores, and I never want you to imagine me holidaying on your bones and keeping pieces of you like souvenirs you don't want me to take. So I thought long and hard about it because shoot, shag or marry isn't something I take lightly. I guess it also did get me thinking about how one day we're all going to end up married with kids and what not, and now I think about how you would probably end up getting back together with Garret and marrying him, and I'll end up marrying some fucking hot Swedish backpacker slash part time model that I plan on meeting at some youth hostel in Barcelona next year. And I know you don't believe me when I say I'm going, but I really am this time. This time's different.

But yeah I was thinking about you marrying Garrett and how when you do we're probably going to have to stop hanging out so much, because Garrett is a cocksucker—I'm sorry, he really is—and I won't be able to hack having him around trying to be all friendly all the time like he does. I guess we'll come visit you guys in Papua New Guinea because you guys will move back there, and you'll come visit us in Sweden because I won't bother sticking around Brisbane if you're not here. I know you can't marry someone who isn't from PNG, because I know how important culture and heritage and things from where you come from are to you, so I guess he's the one. But I wanted to do something because I wanted to cheer you up over this whole Garrett thing, show you that there are still people who care about you even if he doesn't seem to at the moment. And I didn't tell you about it because I feel like every time I tell you about some plan I have it never happens.

I spend hours on the computer, writing down recipes, locating ingredients. I go to the Sunshine Coast to buy banana leaves; you can't buy them here. Not fresh ones, anyway. I drive to Byron—you think I'm going to buy weed from Nimbin which is a fair enough assumption, but it's to buy sago grub and beetle nut, and I buy fish every day from the Riverside markets until I can get it just right, because it has to be perfect, see, it's like your story about Lachlan is always there in the back of my head and I want to show you that some of us don't want to cut pieces out of you, we want to fill them, and if you are going to marry Garrett I need to show you how things should be made for you so that you have the memory up your spine to demand perfection from him. The first time I wrap the fish and rice in the banana leaves like the YouTube video showed me, it falls apart when I take it out of the fire pit I made in the back yard, and the fish is all gross and the rice is filthy, but by the fifth time I get it right, I think, and I bake about 20 yams until they're less like rocks and more like whatever yams should be like. I go to Mum's when she isn't home and steal her silverware, and I watch another YouTube video on how to set a table but I don't bother with candles because I don't want you to think this is some romantic bullshit. It's not like that at all. But suddenly with you standing there in the living room of my shitty apartment, it's fucking stupid, you grew up in PNG and I can't replicate an entire childhood in one week of YouTube tutorials, and you have to marry Garrett because I can only stand in place of a husband when the real thing isn't around.

Garrett left you, you say. Garret doesn't want you anymore, you tell me. You say you can't even eat, that you're too empty to fill up, that you're already full from anger. You say that the dinner looks beautiful and that it was real nice of me to do all of this for you, and that you wish you could enjoy it but that you just can't. I tell you that I understood and normally I would be lying because I never understand why you get upset over Garrett but this time I do, and I put some popcorn into the microwave and we sit on the couch and watch Seinfeld reruns while dinner gets cold behind us. You leave around 9, and I am tired of being hungry all the time, so fucking tired of it, so I sit down at the table across an empty setting and I eat. The fish is like an ocean. The yams are so sweet. I scoop the rice up with pieces of cut coconut and let it crash around my mouth, roll along my tastebuds, and I picture your smile, and I eat more fish and devour the yams and pour coconut down my throat until I've eaten every crumb I can find, licked every drop of lime juice off of the table, and I sit there in front of empty plates, so heavy, stuck in this chair like I've eaten an entire island. A belly full of you, this is the furtherest I have ever travelled from Brisbane. I remember you once told me to stop staring at globes and find 'place blo mipla'—a place that belonged to me. The scary thing is, with a makeshift island behind me, and with popcorn and you on my couch, I felt like I had found it. But I'm going to buy those tickets to Barcelona. I really am this time.

Tell Me

Jake Brain

I genuinely feel endangered anytime I ride shotgun in your car. Go on, tell me to slow down.

Say something about film, about your Palme d'Or collection, you're tired and hungry right? Tell me how Christopher Moltisanti dies the week before I see it. Tell me about the girl you picked up at Pie Face, tell me its wrong to pass a joint to a kid and put it on Facebook.

Don't tell me it's OK for her to be upset, like you'd know, you've never been in a relationship.

My teeth weren't ones to emulate, make sure you tell Tessa. Tell Mum I'm failing Unit, feed me a Mitsubishi and watch me talk Dad's head off. Film me playing a Shooter, then cackle at teenage loneliness, one you shared. Call me immature then throw a rasher of bacon on the floor of a café. Tell me you're not waiting, you're not driving, roll your eyes when I light up.

Make sure I know you love chili, make sure everyone knows you love chili; it's a thing of yours. After mispronouncing chipotle.

Say Happy Birthday and order all the meat. Tell me to do the same.

Tell me I forgot about cash flow, remind me to do it so Dad can do payroll, tell me to meet up if I'm in the city tonight, otherwise Happy Birthday again, tell me to have a great weekend if I don't make it to your new city apartment. Card me, write you're proud of me, you wouldn't ever want another brother in the world, just me, you can't wait to spend the years. Tell me you'll see me on Monday. Tell me, you love me, genuinely, with no awkwardness.

Silence 1,2,3,4,5.

Pull a sickie.

Silence 1,2,3.

Keep a spare key to your apartment in a desk drawer. Tell me to call Dad, tell it not to pick up, tell me to guess. Tell me to run up the slope a ways to your apartment, flashing your buzzer, jamming elevator button number one. Tell me to rock back and forth on your shitty couch, tell me to listen to shrieks, tell *me* to shriek at ambulance drivers and a novice homicide detective. Tell me to apologise afterward… Tell me what the hell to say to Dad…

Silence 1,2.

Tell me to sit in silence in that great iron monstrosity and nod softly. Tell me how to drive past Brighton, Sans Souci, Caringbah, Uncle at the wheel, Dad at shotgun, me in the back, tell me to permit a moments joy on Tessa's face as she sees us returning home early from work.

Tell me to sit silent on another couch.

Silence 1,2,3,4,5.

Tell me you love my first play, like my second, not sure about my third. Avoid our cousins with me. Cheat on your wife, cheat with my wife. You never have to wait again.

Show me Everest. Pack an Everest, pull it, and lose your shit with me. Slice up a hog and drown everyone at Quay in clotted pork blood with me. Cover my backyard in capsicums, en masse, I'll tend them myself; Arbols, ancho's, habanero's, guajillo's, big red peppers. You can call them chipottle's if you want, I'll never correct you again.

Read my writing and tell me, no bullshit, tell me you hate it, tell me you love it, call me a genius. Judge me… Fuck me if you want, I don't care.

Listen to Talking Heads with me. Dance to 'This Must Be the Place' with me. Like you never ruined it.

Rap Kendrick, watch Game and hate LeBron with me. Lets ball, see my new step-back, my behind the back, watch me drain 3's from fucking everywhere mate, watch me kill you.

Be the monster in a pool for our kids with me. Whinge about your wife to me, force them to drive us home every Christmas howling in the backseat, face-timing with me, hire divorce lawyers with me, mid-life crisis with me, Ferrari with me, mount the world with me.

Silence 1,2,3,4,5.

Tell me to never manipulate people with my grief.

Tell me how to repress, to almost forget. Teach me to excise yourself from me.

Tell me you know I love you. Tell me you know I'm sorry, you know I was busy.

Silence 1,2.

Help me be a better brother to our sister, to cherish her, guide her like you did. Marvel with me at the young woman she is and will be. Pop bottles with her boyfriends and me. Approve her husband with me. Protect her. Inspire her. Laugh at her with me.

Silence 1,2,3.

Tell me to say something to Mum, anything, tell me to find strength in hers, tell me she doesn't need silence, she wants me to hold her, hug her, cry on her, show my weakness to her, to be her little boy again…

Silence 1,2,3,4.

Tell me what the hell I say to Dad…

Silence, 1,2.

Tell me I found you instead…

Silence, 1,2.

Tell that aneurysm not today, and not ever.

Silence, 1.

Shake my hand, take my firstborn and cradle her, cherish her.

Watch as our sons become big and little brothers and cousins and suffer through graduations together, Christmases together, wakes together.

Silence 1, 2, 3, 4, 5, 6, 7, 8, 9, 10.

Call surprise, here I am… Tell me I'm dreaming when a cutie walks past, but really, surprise, here's your piece back, me back, I was just holding it in secret for a while, give me a welder, a visor and surprise, we're back together, Frankensteined.

Sweet Sour

Sophie Hardcastle

Sam, a teenager, sorts through a box of loose papers and comes across lemon cake recipe.

For the base,
Melted butter
250 g self-raising flour
Lemon zest
Pinch of salt
200 g castor sugar
250 g unsalted butter
4 large eggs

And for the syrup,
2/3 cup of castor sugar
Juice of one *lemon*…
…*A* lemon.

Pause.

Lemons…

…'Lemons are sweeter than strawberries',

Says she read it on the underside of a bottle cap.

Mum's pockets are full of odd facts—how she remembers pointless shit like that…

Sam is blown away.

'Did you know that?'

Sam shakes head.

Nope.

Beat.

Sweet strawberries, grapes, sliced melons, oranges, blood oranges, apples, mango, banana, all this fruit painting the table like daubs of wet oil on canvas.

And that's only at one end!

Stretching over the other half are hot sausages, toasted sourdough, eggs poached, ham and cheese croissants, potato rostis, scones with jam and cream and a pecan maple Danish...

So much food—too much food... A feast fit for a Queen.

Beat.

Somewhere in the middle of all those trays and bowls is this huge jug of sparkling water, garnished with slices of sour lemon.

A lavish feast fit for a... broken family of five

Beat.

She sits at the head of the table—like a queen should,

Running her hands over the tablecloth. It's her favourite.

We'd pulled it down from the top cupboard and I'd sneezed as I'd shaken the dust off its skin out in the yard. I don't know why she likes it. I think it's rather ugly.

But now it's out, and it's on the table... *where it should be.*

They sit together... Mum and her custard yellow tablecloth, basking in sunshine that drips from the skylight like softened honeycomb.

Beat.

Dad leans over, 'it's a good thing we're all here'.

Sam nods.

It *is* a good thing we're all here. It's a good thing we're all home.

Beat.

I sink my teeth into a slice of sourdough, topped with a poached egg and hollandaise, and I think that's the moment—right there—egg yoke oozes over my lips—mum slams down her knife and fork.

That is the moment sweet mayonnaise turns sour.

Mum grins at me.

'I know who you are!'

Dad spits chewed up strawberry scone into a napkin.

The three of us kids watch his face curdle the same way it had when a car dealership rang to say his wife was trying to buy a Porsche with her credit card.

Everyone is silent.

'You're Katie'

Sam takes a deep breath.

My name is Sam.

Blake's out of his chair, 'You've got to be kidding me'

Please son.

'It's fucking mother's day and my mum's not even *here*'

For most people the sight of a twenty-four year old boy crying is rare, but I get it. It's different for him. It's different for him *and* Tess.

They were older.

They understood the tragedy of a mum who couldn't get out of bed on dark days… a mum who waited at the school gates for the wrong kids.

I was young… oblivious… Lucky maybe.

'You're my little sister'

Tess's tears are seeping into the custard tablecloth.

'We were split up, you and I'

Mum's smile is cherry sauce in a stale puff pastry.

And all *I* can think about is the night she'd crept into my room and sat on my bed. How she'd wiped my wet cheeks on her sleeve and how I'd begged her to stay. Over and over and over I begged my silent silhouette to stay.

But she said nothing.

Beat.

Maybe that's because there just aren't any words for a mother who takes her child's hand and places it on her stomach in the dark.

Beat.

At the time I hadn't known why there were so many wrinkles in the cotton.

I hadn't known the way psychosis could turn a mind on its body.

I hadn't known the way mania could make time pass quicker or the way depression could make time stop all together.

I was nine... how could I have possibly known the way sour thoughts could convince hands to ravage their own sweet skin?

We'd just sat there, Mum and me... I don't know for how long, but we'd just sat there, on my bed, beneath the creamy glow of a nightlight with my hand resting on her *scored* belly.

Beat.

For weeks after she left, I'd sobbed, right up until my birthday arrived with a lemon cake.

No one ate it of course. He'd messed up the recipe. Dad had messed up *Mum's* recipe.

The bin swallowed ten candles, a burnt base and a tart, yellow icing.

Beat.

Mum's looking at me now over the mountain of food, literally *right* at me.

I swear to god, nothing compares to this feeling... to have someone look at you, but not see you.

She takes a sip of water. And as her dark irises melt on my face, a slice of lemon touches her lip.

'I had to run away to see you... And I did, because you're my sister.'

No one's brave enough to stop the queen as she rises from her throne.

No ones brave enough to even move.

'You're my *beautiful* little sister, and look at you!

Goose bumps prickle.

She's standing over my shoulder.

Goose bumps sting.

She's stroking my hair.

Sam plays with hair.

MY HAIR! As if these short brown tufts are *thick* mango locks.

'*So* gorgeous.'

She kisses my forehead. My cheek. She lingers. She whispers.

'I'm so proud of you'

Peach perfume burns my nose.

Fermented words burn my throat.

Beat.

Holding my face like a sausage between crusty sourdoughs. Her smile is as sweet as it is sour.

'I love you... little sister'

Five words

Choking on three

Gagging on two

I bite my tongue so hard I taste blood.

Beat.

Mum's hand is on my shoulder and before any of us realise what's going on, she's kicked her leg up and slammed it down on the plate of ham and cheese croissants.

'You've still got a way to go little sister!' she laughs, 'These are pretty big boots to fill!'

Long pause.

I don't know why I crack up, but I do.

And then Tess starts laughing, *and* Dad.

We don't even try to help her in her sick state of delusion because her laugh is raw. We just sit there, drenched in yellow light as she dances on this smooth butter cloud.

Soon my mouth hurts and I've got this awful stitch in my stomach because I can't control this hysteria.

Beat.

Landing her foot on the ground, Mum wipes my wet cheeks with her sleeve, takes this deep drawn-out breath, and gazes over the table,

'This is a good moment... isn't it?'

Pause.

I look around at my family. This is the most tragic and yet the most beautiful thing I have ever seen.

Pause.

Did *you* know lemons have more sugar than strawberries?

Pause.

I take her hand...

'I love you too big sister.'

My words are as sweet as they are sour.

Sweet in the Savoury

Tasnim Hossain

A young woman in a headscarf enters and begins to speak to an unseen friend.

That first time we cook together, who is it who comes up with the idea? It must be you.

Hell, frypans and I are *not* friends. I'm surprised that I agree.

But before I know it, there we are, eco bags in hand, in amongst the stroller pushing mums.

We're searching for recipes on your iPad in a deli. Which is so deliciously ironic. I can't eat pork, you're vegetarian, and we're googling quinoa recipes surrounded by salami.

We find a recipe. Eventually. Spend hours tramping up and down the aisles of a bunch of different supermarkets. Searching for the right ingredients.

An adventure.

That's what it is.

A quest for the perfect meal.

We take turns pushing the trolley. We look like we are together and I can't tell if that makes me feel uncomfortable or not.

Pause.

That first lunch is at your house, and I don't realise it at the time, but I think it is the start of us.

We are kindred spirits.

You recognise the same sadness in me.

I think that I have been broken, but you know that I am just bruised. But you don't say anything.

You just invite me over to cook.

Beat.

We get to yours with loaded shopping bags and you give me a heads up as we walk in the door.

She speaks as her friend.

'My grandmother's staying here. She doesn't have very long. She sleeps a lot and might forget you right after she meets you.'

I nod. I love grandmothers.

My *dadi* was always too far away. The Indian Ocean is pretty big. Too big to cross just to eat the fish and eggplant curries my father reminisces about.

Beat.

Perhaps it's just as well. She'd probably think it was about time I got married. Set me up with one of my cousins or something.

Pause.

I meet your mother and sister. Your aunt and cousin. A house filled with women. All but you. They sit and talk and move quietly. Bear witness.

Beat.

When I next see you, she is gone.

It's been less than a week.

There's nothing left of her except the boxes of baking trays and pans, the new mixer, the old cookbooks.

They wait for you. She wanted you to have them.

You told me once that she was the one who taught you how to make sweet things for the ones you love.

And that's what you do.

Beat.

You teach me.

We bake together, you and I. We try new things.

Those salted caramel cupcakes? The ones, that waltz across our tongues. We eat the frosting straight out of the bowl. I swear that there is at least half a kilo of butter in that.

Actually, no. Don't think about it. Why ruin something that was so good? I hate that.

I hate it when people describe eating as sinful or naughty. To not savour every bite, now *that* is a sin.

That's the same day we make the wasabi and white chocolate ones, right? You ask me how they are.

'It's... an experience.'

Beat.

I'm being generous.

We end up with sixty cupcakes. And between four people in your household and four people in mine, somewhere the maths has gone wrong.

My mother expresses a vague concern about it. All the time spent alone with a boy, a white boy. I just laugh.

You cook me tajines and I eat sweet in the savoury, something I had never liked before. But honeyed chickpeas taste perfect off your spoon.

We throw parties and I tell you that you must be ethnic, because you invite ten and make enough for forty.

Pause.

You know your watermelon salad? The one with mint and feta? The first time you serve it, I think you're taking the piss. Funny that. It's still my favourite.

Now when we go grocery shopping, you take my hand, and I'm not afraid of belonging with you the way I am with everyone else.

I start to learn how to cook. Imperceptibly. Accidentally. Before meeting you, I could make three things. Pizza. Lasagne. Spaghetti bolognaise. Cooking Italian was my teenage rebellion.

I never learnt the... formula? The dance. The dance of spices that scent the memories of my childhood. By the time I was 14, I hated it. I hated going to school smelling likechillieslikebay leaveslikecinnamonlikecardamomlikecorianderlikecuminlike cloves.

Beat.

Like curry.

Besides, every time a girl in my community makes something even vaguely edible, I know the teasing from the aunties that always follows. Always.

'Oh, you can cook now, can you? Time to find you a husband.'

It's meant to be a joke.

Beat.

Eventually, I realise that I want to cook for you. I want you to taste the love a Bangladeshi mother feeds her children every night.

You know, I never told you this, but the night before, I spent an hour and a half on the phone with my mum, adjusting recipes.

Potatoes in place of meat.

Half a teaspoon of turmeric to one and a half cauliflowers.

Green lentils, overnight. Yellow lentils, ready to cook.

Toast the masala on low heat until fragrant.

The first time I cook for us, you come over early so we can prepare the meal together, as we always have. For the first time, you are sous chef, and I tell you what to do.

You'd always been egalitarian. Me, I'm a tyrant.

I make you chop all the onions and chillies because I hate doing it. You don't complain.

It's pretty great.

You leave me frying it all off in mustard seed oil to go to the bathroom and when you return, there is nobody around. Empty kitchen. The acrid stench of burnt food.

You can't find me. You know something is wrong.

You move around the kitchen. You call my name.

I shift. I bump against a sack of rice. It's only a little rustle but you hear.

You open the pantry door. Light floods in.

And I'm rocking. Back and forth. Back and forth.

And the tears drip, drip, soak my scarf.

It's shit. It's shit. I'm shit.

I will never be a good cook.

I will never be a good wife.

I will never be a good person.

I will never

I will never

I will never

Be

Enough.

Beat.

Never.

Pause.

You put your arms around me.

You smell like grapefruit handwash.

You kiss me on the forehead.

You tell me that I was always going to make a shit housewife anyway.

I laugh.

I can't help it.

I laugh and laugh and we scrape together what we can salvage and we sit down to dinner and while we eat, we laugh.

Beat.

It is not the best aloo gobi I have tasted.

It won't be the best aloo gobi I make.

But it is enough.

So... thank you.

Beat.

I promise I'll make a better one some other time.

When you're free.

One that doesn't taste like ashes.

Long pause.

That first meal we cooked at your place, the quinoa salad we planned in a deli, I couldn't believe that you had trusted me with something as precious as your family. Me, who was still basically a stranger.

I think we both quietly hoped that sweet indulgences and nourishing food would mend our broken hearts. Fill our bellies. With anything, other than bitterness.

For me, over a man with gentle eyes and bear-like hands. For you, a man with a cocky grin and Freddie Mercury's face.

I know now that the blue-eyed bear will never be mine, but your chiselled-cheekboned Freddie finally seems to be waking up to the wonder of you. I wish you both all the joy in the world.

You two will be good together.

Pause.

I don't know. Maybe hearts never really heal.

But friends, and watermelon salad, make a lot of difference.

Silence. Lights fade.

Something I Prepared Earlier

Julian Larnach

David walks onto an empty soundstage in an apron and a chef's hat. An oversized novelty boom mike hangs over his head: not visible at first, it lowers over the course of the piece.

Silence

David Food is…

Pause.

Oh.

I've prepared a few ways it could…

Oh.

Great.

Just keep going.

You'll say when to…

Stop. Got it.

Oh, I didn't see the…

He moves onto an X made of adhesive tape on the ground.

Pause.

I feel like James Bond.

You know?

Staring down the barrel of the…

He starts humming the James Bond theme song, really gets into it.

Lights down.

David clears his throat.

Lights up.

Food is fuel. Simple, really. You eat crap, you'll feel crap. You feel crap, you'll… *be* crap. It's a vicious cycle but the best way to break a cycle is at the beginning. I'm talking breakfast, people—yeah!

Say bye bye to bacon. Ta-ta to toast. See you later Chip-o-lata. And welcome to your lips and to your life... BRAN!

It might not be considered traditionally as... pucker tucker but it's high in fibre. And fibre helps you... yep, that's right. And what's better than... ? Nothing!

Goes to high-five someone, realises the audience is quite far away.

Your body is a well-oiled machine but sometimes if it's less than optimally oiled you'll break down on the highway of life.

Too far with the fuel analogy?

Well yes.

I mean, no.

I've got my Ls. Right.

Well I've also got...

Art.

Right?

Pause.

Food is art. And you, dear viewer, you are the artist. Your canvas, the plate. Your paint box, the kitchen closet. Your easel, the...

Too arty?

I can dial back the...

Right.

Pause.

Food is... sport. Food is sport. Tonight I'm going to show you how to stuff a turkey with a goose with a chicken with a duck with a guinea fowl with a teal with a woodcock with a patridge with a plover with a lapwing with a quail with a thrust with a lark with an ortolan bunting with a garden warbler. The Romans called it dinner. The French call it *roti sans pareil*—the incomparable roast. The Americans call it a Turducken. I can call it the turkoosekenuck guineal woodidger lapailustark ortolarber.

Pause.

Why?

What would you call it?

Pause.

Food is...

David puts his hands on his hips.

Sex.

Pause.

Noted. Never, *ever* again.

Food is adventure, yeah! While most people request a New Zealand chardonnay from their local bar, I'd rather be guzzling snake piss in South-East Asia.

Maybe an evening of salsa dancing with your boyfriend sounds like a great night out. I'd rather be dancing with the devil as I sample the poisonous delight of Japanese pufferfish.

I'm going to teach you how to fry spiders in Cambodia, find witchetty grubs in the outback and how to *hunt, kill* and *strip* the heart out of a live Icelandic puffin.

No? We don't have the budget to... yeah I get that, it is quite far away. I just thought that maybe... I thought maybe we could do a bake sale or a raffle. Raffles are a bona fide way to...

Oh, too gross? Too gross.

Pause.

Well, well maybe you're just not ready, huh?

Not brave enough, huh?

Not *man* enough to push your taste buds to the culinary limit!

Pause.

No? Okay, here we go. I think you'll really...

David clears his throat, puffs out chest and starts pacing back and forth.

Food is war. Pigs are the enemy. Pork is your prize. Evolution has granted us opposable thumbs in our war against our porcine hoofed antagonists. If you think for a second that a pig wouldn't slaughter you in your sleep if it was given the chance—given *half* a chance—

you are wrong, dear viewer. You are wrong. It would force you into a cage. It would tie your legs to the corners of the aforementioned cage and it would feed you through a tube, and it would make you *poop* through a tube and you would grow fat, *grotesquely* fat. It would collect your young. And this is your life, do you want me to say how you would be killed for your new pig overlords?

No, no. I'm not saying…

No, not any pigs I'd use.

I assure you sir, that I would only use free-range pigs.

They would live in a meadow.

Well, lived.

They would have *lived* in a meadow.

Where? I… I don't know but I've been assured it was pleasant.

Pause.

Please, sir I've got a few to…

Food is science!

Pause.

David's eyes slowly widen.

Food.

Is.

…

God?

He sits down.

I can do this. I can, just give me a…

Food is…

I don't know. I don't know what you want.

Sorry, I…

Pause. David stands up and begins to walk away.

Food is…

Good.

David stops and turns around.

I like it, food.

I eat it, food.

I help cook it when I'm asked to or when I can.

I don't want the thing I'm eating to be in pain but I also want hamburgers.

I don't need my meal to take eighty hours to prepare but I don't want something that took longer to eat than it did to cook. I want to put chicken salt on my chips—even though I'm sure there's no chicken, and pretty sure there's no salt in it. But equally, I don't want to die of a heart attack. I would really, really *not* like to die of a heart attack.

I think food should be fun and simple but if it needs to it should be serious and have a stupidly long list of hard-to-find ingredients because that's how mum makes it and that's how I want it to taste. I'm not being snooty, I'm being picky for the *right* reasons.

It should... it should make memories. You remember the joke your dad told when he was serving the roast potatoes at Christmas, you *don't* remember the carb count.

Food is important because... the way we want our food to be is the way we want our friends, our family, our*selves*... to be.

Pause.

Sorry, I've wasted your time. I'll just...

He goes to leave.

Pause.

He stops.

Really?

That was...

You don't want anymore...

Great.

Yeah.

I can do after 4.

I've got school.

Yeah it does end at 3.

I mean I could come earlier but I've got afternoon tea.

That's not a problem, is it?

Lights down.

Is it?

Dig In Dean

Zac Linford

Note: When the text is in bold, the family can hear it, diegetic.

Tess is at a table.

Sit here Dean.

It'll be fine.

It'll be fine. They'll love him. Dad's got a drink. Chris is into the chips, too busy to talk that's good. Dean's alright? Buttoned up his shirt. Good good. **Roast lamb. This looks excellent Mum. Thanks a lot. Well, dig in Dean. Don't wait for us,** [*Beat.*] don't wait for us. I hope everyone likes him. I hope they don't fucking embarrass me. I'll just eat and after dinner we can go to my room and make out or something.

She eats very quickly, shovelling the food into her mouth. She stops when she catches sight of Dean.

He is just starting on the beans? [*Beat.*] He's bringing the fork to his mouth so slowly, so incredibly slowly with one skewered bean on it. One! He's not even leaning closer to the plate. It's the simplest thing in the world. [*Beat.*] How have I not noticed this before? Why doesn't he just sit with his head jutting out over the plate? You can bring the food in quicker and if any falls off your fork or out of your mouth it doesn't even matter. It just lands right back into where it belongs. Look at me Dean, look. See this? This is how you eat. Look at all of us. We are all eating like this. Just look.

It's fine. It'll be fine. So he doesn't eat as fast as us. It's fine. It's Dean. He has had some of the potatoes, I can be thankful for that at least. [*Beat.*] Although, completely out of order. It should be greens first, then that oniony tomatoey bread-crumby thing that Mum makes, then the pumpkin then you divide your time between the meat and potatoes, ask anyone. It's one thing at a time. That's how we're all doing it. Look at Chris, he's doing it Dean, why can't you?

On our very first date he brought his brother along and bought all of us tickets. It was really weird, like he was trying to set me up with his brother for some reason. Or like I'd just third wheeled their bro-time. So he bought a big thing of popcorn and there was still some left at the end. [*Beat.*] At the end. [*Beat.*] He didn't start eating until after the previews finished. I mean, who has the patience for that? [*Beat.*] Oh thank fuck, he's finished the beans. Quick move on, next thing. Oh, look Dean, Dad has already finished his dinner. He always finishes first.

Dean, c'mon, you're letting me down. How the hell am I meant to be with you when you can't keep up with me or my family? Jesus, I need the blender or a funnel or something to force this down you. Oh, now Chris has finished his. It's not like I want you to be more like Chris or Dad or anything it's just, Jesus, I mean, you haven't even finished the onion thing. You're talking way too much, that's what it must be. Mum's asking too many questions.

Tess looks for the right moment to interrupt the conversation.

Um Chris, how's Emily? Good that should work for a little bit. Get him to the end of the pumpkin at least. Focus Dean, focus, force it down. No, what are you– why are you getting involved? You don't even know Emily. Shit, um, **yeah well that's a good point I suppose, what do you think Chris? Mum? Dad?** Dean, eat your fucking food. [*Beat.*] Look now Mum's almost finished too. This is getting so embarrassing. How have I not noticed this yet? We've eaten together before [*Beat.*] when we went to the tapas place [*Beat.*] with the really small servings… I don't know why I thought it was cute, it's fucking weird.

Can you only fit in small mouthfuls at a time? Like the mouth of a chicken but without the beak and plus lips and teeth but small ones not like a gerbil or a snake so you can only get in a little bit at a time. Like some kind of weird pellet eating chicken man mouth thing. Is that what you are Dean? Is it? [*Beat.*] **Can you pass the mint jelly? No no Dean, don't worry about it. I'll get it, you eat.**

What are my parents gonna think of you, if you can't even get down a lamb roast? If you don't finish this meal soon Dean, Dad will get his shotgun. Do you feel this? This pressure I'm sending to you telepathically? [*Beat.*] Okay, he doesn't really have a shotgun but I'm just trying to help. My family won't respect you. How can they when you can't even finish the pumpkin? Mum's pumpkin is a one bite kind of thing. You may not know this Dean, but my Mum grew up in a very poor household. As she was the youngest of eight, if she didn't eat fast, she didn't eat. You're basically just spitting in the face of my childhood mother. Right in her face, Dean. We all eat fast now. It's bred into us, like prized greyhounds.

Tess stands up to look over Dean's shoulder.

Why can't you do this? I like you Dean, I really do, but what if we have kids? What if they turn out to be freakish slow eaters like you? Tiny chicken man mouthed babies. [*Beat.*] Mum's finished now Dean. How long are you going to have to sit here? Do we have to wait for you for the rest of the night as you chop up those tiny pieces of meat? Just fold it over and whack the whole thing in your mouth.

Why did I think we were ready for this? I mean, I think I love you Dean but, Dad's judging you now. Look, he's got that stance ready like he's about to launch an attack. I hate it when he does that. He doesn't even give you a chance to respond properly. And its usually quite racist stuff. Dad's a bit old fashioned that way, very old fashioned actually. But at least he can fucking finish a meal–

No way, they are the smallest portions of meat I have ever seen. How can you even chew on that? Who has precise enough teeth to even get close? This is so incredibly awkward. Chris isn't even looking at you now Dean and Mum's just doing her own thing.

Tess slumps back into her chair.

Yes? What is it Dean? I see you looking at me. What?

Beat.

I see you.

Beat.

I see you smile.

Beat.

and on my fork is a potato *and* a bean [*pause*] and popcorn and tapas and meat and onions and movies and your new buttoned up shirt.

Beat.

And we eat.

Beat.

And we look at each other.

Beat.

And we eat.

Beat.

And then, we've finished, together. And put our forks down. [*Beat.*]
Are you up for seconds?

Facon

Felicity Pickering

A plastic wrapped stack of 'Stop Animal Suffering' pamphlets sits beside a rotisserie. A pair of tongs lay on the pamphlets resting on paper towels. The tongs are charred and used. The rotisserie has a few fake flowers stuck to it roughly with sticky tape. The rotisserie provides the thick scent of meat and metal. Ti enters. She has blonde dreadlocks scooped up in a scrunchie and is wearing a PETA shirt and Thai fisherman pants.

Meat.

Red dripping, mailed by the kilo, barbeque sizzling.

Hold it on your face after you whacked your head, meat.

A little too rare. Pink in the middle. Who's watching the steaks?
Meat.

Wagu, New York, two-minute steak. Veal, venison, hear the crackling break.

Boutique bangers with rosemary and lamb, cherry pinned and decorated,

'It's Christmas day' ham!

The muscle that holds our family together is meat.

My friend once said that she had never come over without there being a two-minute steak defrosting in the oven. I've always been an animal caring type, but in a house that hates to cook, but can work a BBQ, it's hard to survive on chickpeas and lentils.

I've tried before. I attempted being straight vegetarian when I was overseas: I chose the falafel over the kebab; the veggie wrap over the deep fried chicken, but nothing feels more like home than a little French mustard and a rare steak.

It was a reality I had to accept. I was a meat eater, born and braised. But that's not the kind of thing you can admit to these days. See... I hang with theatre types, militant hipsters and a Surry Hills crowd. And with these kinds of kids eating meat ain't allowed.

To survive in the cut throat climate of the urban hip,

I had to control how I'd appear. So I covered my carnivorous core with a vegan veneer.

I went to extreme measures to maintain this façade. I was strictly vegan in public. I always wore hash. I had 'I stop for animals' stuck on the back of my car. I was fluent in veganese. I knew my chia seeds from chickpeas, my boca burgers from black beans and kale from quinoa.

Meat was a primal pleasure indulged in private, and glazed over at dinner parties. I had my story down pact . It was easy to live this lie until my father decided we should 'stop going through the middle man' and get our own meat.

Suddenly fire pits sprouted up in the backyard and spit roasters were stored on the tiles by the side path. The smokey aroma of ham, mixed with charcoal and spices, hung like a mushroom cloud over the house, bringing foxes and rats out from the undergrowth. I was burning ten incense sticks a day to keep the smell of bacon off my *textile recycled* clothing.

Being in the office was a nightmare. Here I was sitting at my desk at a sustainable living charity, writing blog post after blog post about how we should become vegetarian to save the planet, and just hoping that no-one could smell the salami stuck under my nails.

The façade was becoming too much.

The idea of a humanitarian friend making an impromptu visit made my heart race. Could I put flowers on the spit roaster and call it an avant-garde art work? Could the meat hooks be for artistic ambience… like in the Meatpacking District of Soho? Perhaps for a short story I was writing?

Pause.

But what about the pig pen in the backyard?

I was having nightmares where I would come into work, go into a meeting, and suddenly they would all be staring at me and I would realise I was dressed in a Lady Gaga meat dress. Next they would strap me to the very same spit roast that I'd stick taped flowers to. Then they would eat me, piece by piece and they would say that it was ethical, because I needed to know how the animals felt.

I didn't think it would be a problem for James though, at first. He was just an easy-going guy. I met him at Linley Park, near the scouts' hall. I saw him standing there alone flying a kite.

I asked. 'Do like to get high?'

And I seduced him from there.

He liked me because I wasn't like the people in this peninsula, as insular as the geographic location. He liked that I was into saving the environment, into politics, hated Tony Abbott and into… that I was a vegan.

I didn't ever say I was a vegan. It was almost like he assumed. Well actually it went a little like this:

Are you a vegan?

Everyone is vegan these days.

See it wasn't a lie, really.

See I never really *said* I was a vegan. He just kind of assumed.

I'd sit in the office and dream of him, fighting off offers for vegan moose.

I hate it when vegans say 'this tastes like the real thing'. Avocado isn't chocolate moose okay? You just haven't had chocolate moose for so long that you've forgotten what it tastes like.

But messages from James were a savoured distraction. I'd sit there thinking of James' thighs stretched out and our taut bodies marinating in each other. Me dousing him in my saucy side and allowing his burly beef to infuse with my full bodied flavour.

But the human abattoir that was my house wasn't settling down. What had started as the work of an amateur hobbyist had become a full grown obsession. Dad had decided it was unfair on the pigs to be using a guillotine. A gas chamber was the only humane way to do it. I'd sit in my bed listening to the snorts of the pigs and the chainsaw whirling late into the night.

I could tell James and I were getting *really* serious when he gave me an anklet made of pins and mud beads. That is like a 4 Carrot Gold necklace for a hippy.

It was a Sunday night when the situation reached boiling point. I was just about to tuck into a lamb back strap, with a duck entrée, when my Dad asks:

'So, Tia pet, who's this new boyfriend of yours?'

'Just a guy.'

'Your birthday's coming up. Why don't you invite him over.'

'No I cannot FUCKING INVITE HIM ALRIGHT?'

Parents. Am I right? So controlling! But it wasn't just Dad who was getting this idea. James was the same.

'Why do you always come to my house? You know, I'd really love to meet your parents.'

So sweet, so kind. Bless him.

'I hope you're not ashamed of me.'

He didn't even realise the bloody mess that he'd gotten involved in. It wasn't his fault. So I invited him over, I KNOW!

It was stupid of me and I guess on some level *I knew* that he'd never believe that my parents were performance artists who used the carcasses of bodies as a political statement against…

But I just hoped he would. I just hoped he liked me enough to swallow down every lie I fed him and he would *pretend* to believe me. And that it would be an unspoken betrayal, like a fart on a first date, something that's uncomfortable at the time, but would be laughed about later. To bring it on my *birthday* would just be in bad taste!

Beat.

I greeted him at the front door. He was dressed in his best khaki shorts and a smart shirt from Nimbin. He'd gotten me another present.

A copy of *The Life Aquatic.*

You are such a good present giver.

I led him to the side area.

I hoped he'd be so distracted by Mum's hugs or Dad's offering of birthday cupcakes that he wouldn't see the zebra (dad had gotten real creative this year), slowing rotating in the middle. But I could see his face contorting into one of disgust. I pulled him to the backyard, bypassing the pig pen. I was starting to smell death in the air and it wasn't just the pigs this time. All blood had drained from his features.

[To an imaginary James] James, I love you. And I don't want an imitation of you, because together our love is raw and real and I feel like I have constructed a skeleton of what our lives would be together and it's not something I want to give up.

We compliment each other like turkey and cranberry sauce. I know it seems I presented a façade but there is some truth in there, and truth I can't argue with, I do love animals. I think public transport is the future. I vote for the greens. I love to boycott! But I can't keep pretending I'm something I'm not.

I am a meat eater. And that doesn't mean we can't be together. I genuinely feel we could be one of the great meat, non-meat combinations of all time: barbeque chicken and tabbouleh, ham and pineapple, fish and chips, bangers and mash.

But he didn't have a bar of it. He felt ambushed and humiliated, and he just said to me:

'It's meat or me, baby. My flesh or theirs.'

And I said:

'Don't say that James, this love is rare.'

He said:

'Don't flog a dead horse, you know this is done.'

And I said:

'Don't do this James. I think you're the one!'

And he just looked at me like I was an animal. He up and left me alone, and I just cried into my steak.

Eating Sunshine

Emily Sheehan

Jess is 17. She stands in Stefan's kitchen in his family home in the Hills district, Sydney. Summertime. It is hot.

JESS I'm not a nice person. I'm not a thoughtful, intelligent, kind, human being who wants the best for the people I care about. I just—I don't know. I don't care I guess. I don't really care enough about myself, or anyone really, to take the time to think about the bigger picture. And I'm not being negative or self-depreciating or whatever, I'm just trying to tell the truth here. This was never a good idea. Obviously. This whole situation we're in is so fucking dumb. But it wasn't my job to stop you. I'm not the one with shit to lose.

Beat.

It's funny how when you're sitting in the thick of life, like really in the thick of it, in the truth of the world as it actually exists, and it's like BAM! Something that was cool and sexy and fun, can suddenly seem like the worst idea you've ever had in your life.

I don't know what I'm saying…

On the train ride over I was reading this article about some guy in the Ukraine who eats sunshine. Literally. I'm not trying to be funny, that is actually what he eats. He 'consumes spatial energy in place of organic matter'. Some Japanese production company made a documentary about him, and he was legit. It works like this: when we eat vegetables we're kind of eating sunshine. Well we're eating vegetables, but what do the vegetables eat? Carbon dioxide plus water plus sunshine equals carbohydrate. Photosynthesis. Plant food, right? So it makes sense. This guy stands in the sun for thirteen hours every day soaking up the rays, living off nothin' but sunshine.

What the hell, right? I don't even know why I'm telling you this. It just seemed significant. Stupid I guess. Plus if I ever tried something like that it would definitely, one hundred percent Go. To. Shit. In fact—in all seriousness—I'd probably die. Just drop dead. Right there in the Ukraine with a Japanese film crew recording the whole thing. And I don't want to fuck up to that extreme. And I didn't mean to fuck things up this bad. I don't even know how it got this far. We're just bad people I guess. You and me; not nice people. It's like I have absolutely no idea what I want so I just go along with whatever comes at me, but it's different this time, because you're, like, old. Well, old enough that you're not on Facebook. Un-stalk-ably old.

No—Listen! When you agreed to go out with me, I couldn't believe it. First of all—unexpected. And before anything even happened just the whole idea was... exciting. I felt superior to those bitches at school. And even though you were married, I didn't give a shit. I actually kinda liked it. This is embarrassing, and call me a horrible person or whatever, but taking someone away from someone else is... I dunno. That's power. You know? Being the other woman. It's validating.

Beat.

Is that her on the fridge? It is, isn't it? No offence, but that's a really bad photo. Sorry. That was rude. I mean it's not that bad. It's just, like, why would you put that photo on the fridge? I'm sure there are way nicer ones where she looks pretty... Dammit, where was I? Oh yeah; validating.

Pause.

You know that lunatic in the Ukraine could die tomorrow. The sunshine guy, remember? He's starving to death and no one gives a shit. Why isn't anyone trying to help him? People just want to film him like some animal in a documentary. It really makes me sick. Someone who loves him needs to tell him he's crazy.

And standing here in your kitchen with fucking photos of your fucking wife on the fucking fridge is weird! I know I said I was fine, but I feel totally uncomfortable! Plus this house it totally depressing so no wonder she wants to kill herself. Sorry. That was rude. I'm just— Like you texting me when that happened was like 'fuck! I don't want to hear that'. I don't want to hear that shit! I'm seventeen years old, what the hell am I supposed to do with that information? What am I supposed to feel about that? Don't make that something I now need to have feelings for! I'm already stressed out enough by us and school and this weirdo Ukranian who I've never met, I don't need your wife's shit on top of that.

And I know about—

I need to tell you that—

Okay I know this will sound completely 1984, but I googled your son last night. He's my age. I found an album on Facebook that he was tagged in and, no offence, but he looks like a stoner. He's a drop kick. An absolute loser. The kind of boy I would *never* be friends with. And I know that's the door to his bedroom, I peeked while you were peeing, and that doesn't make me a crazy person, I was just being thorough.

And I can't shake this stupid image of that sun eater! I'm on the train on the way here—the ticket was like $8 by the way—and this Ukrainan man's staring up at me from my shitty newspaper and I'm like 'what the FUCK am I doing?!?' I'm not this person. I can't handle this. I'm not exciting. I've never even had an STI. And it's making me sad now because it's actually a really beautiful image. A man living off nothing but sunshine. The idea of it seems really super wholesome and grounded and simple. Really simple.

But he's totally lethargic. He has no energy. He does nothing with his days. He's so malnourished that he just lies there. It's gross. It's pathetic.

You seemed beautiful and really super different, but now I'm standing here, staring at the door to your son's bedroom, and I'm shitting my pants, praying that your wife doesn't come home on her lunch break, and you just seem... completely... regular. And all of a sudden being the other woman isn't sexy. It's just sad. And I'm not special. I never was. I thought I was something that could fill you up. Inspire you and satisfy you and fill you up like sunshine. But that Ukrainian man isn't full. He's empty. Literally. I don't mean empty in the figurative sense of the word. His insides are completely empty and sunshine won't fill them up. And I can't fill you up. This is warm and light and beautiful like sunshine, but it won't fill you up.

I'm sorry–

It's–

A breath.

Can you drive me home now? We don't have to talk about it. And you don't need to say sorry or anything. I just think I'd like to go home.

That Daniel

Joel Tan

Daniel in his kitchen. Foot propped up on a chair.

DANIEL Oww oww oww!

What is this *PAIN*?

Fuck this shit.

I'm 21 years old and I've just been diagnosed with a disease that was uncool even in the 19th century.

When I googled it, I got taken to the Wikipedia page, and, to give you a sense of exactly how fucking antiquated this disease is, the one picture they have up is an 18th century rendering of a little demon imp gnawing at some fat man's foot. I'm 21 and I have a disease that's so *uncool*, it hasn't changed its profile picture in 200 years.

Apparently, I'm no longer supposed to drink. Or smoke. Or, for that matter, eat soybeans, but fuck that. [*He takes a swig of whiskey.*] *Ow.*

Most people will probably think I had this coming, but for the wrong reason. I mean, this is a rich man's disease, right? The kind of disease that's sent from heaven to smite the shit out of overfed aristocrats for not sharing. It's a socialist disease. And to that extent, I'm probably in good company: here, I'm thinking Napoleon, Julius Caesar, Liberace.

People might think I deserve this because I consider myself an epicurean, I think I'm pretty smart about food. I have a reputation, I think, for having a highly-evolved taxonomical knowledge of French sauces. I have a relationship with butter. I know how to cook eggs in at least six shocking ways, and that's just *boiling*. You'd think this disease is the dark shadow hiding about my eating habits, the *nemesis* that sprung out of my veins when I made a Faustian blood pact with goose-fat; this disease is my doing *and* undoing.

But, like I said, that's the wrong reason. It'd be easier if that were all true, if the pain were punishment for being an educated glutton. It'd be so much easier to actually deserve this.

No, it's cuz I've been *Meager.* I've been *meager* with myself. I'm being punished for being *meager* with myself. For eating lettuce when I was actually thinking of butter, for tea-spooning boiled soybeans in my mouth while I imagined bowlfuls of steaming carbohydrate. I'll always remember that listless tomato salad on day-one-meal-one of my no-carb diet. I hear a crunching echoing through time, on one hand of cheap iceberg lettuce, which is an abomination, and on the other, of profound, empty hunger grating against determination. 'You've been eating too much soy,' the doctor said with the kind of medical indifference that always takes your drama down a few pegs. 'Too much protein, stop doing that.' I've gotten a disease of excess from an excess of healthy food.

The fact of the matter is that I was once 20kg heavier than I am now. That Daniel, the one with the too-round cheeks, too chubby arms, too profound tummy, too lumbering gait, two touching thighs... he would've enjoyed this disease. It would've made sense, it would've been part of the package, a jokey anecdote to tell at dinner parties, it would've been a kind of badge of honour. A painful badge of honour, but worn with defiance. He would've just kept eating.

'You've not truly lived,' he might say, *'you've not truly lived until you've eaten to animal fullness, eaten to that kind of fullness that renders you catatonic from the mixed pain and pleasure of a belly about to burst, skin taut, eyes dilated, blood rich with sugar, good sense migrated into the clawing, primal, slack-jawed need to eat and taste and eat and taste, and in the eating and the tasting, become aware of the limitations of your body and soul.'*

And he would've meant it. He wouldn't have passed it off, the way I do, as some kind of fancy theoretical flourish to put on paper or Facebook or Twitter or a food blog. He would've said that attended by a shamelessly large bowlful of pasta, sensibly dressed with melted butter and Parmesan cheese, or a plate of pork belly braised with soy sauce and vinegar, swimming darkly in its own rendered juices, or a hunk of fresh-baked bread, still singing from the oven, cracking with a speech of its own, eaten with nothing but a gliding of hand-beaten French butter, flecked with salt and tasting of the sun, earthy and divine.

Beat.

Anthony said:

'You're too fat. I can't love you, you're too fat. I want to but I can't.'

That Daniel, he sat there, cradling a tumbler of gin and tonic. F-a-t, 'fat,' the way the word spat out of Ant's mouth, never mind that the club was so loud his voice was swallowed up. Never mind that the first time you stick your heart out to say 'please love me,' it should be cradled, nursed, like a tumbler of gin and tonic. It was *that* Daniel's first drink in his first gay club.

'Daniel. You're too fat. If you lost… if you lost, I dunno, 15kg, yah, 15kg, then maybe, *maybe* I could.'

That *Daniel*, I think in that moment, in the shattering of strobe lights and the thumping of Kylie, in the bowels of a gay club in Clarke Quay, Singapore, Southeast Asia, the world, the universe, I think that *Daniel* died that night.

Beat.

I remember thinking a lot about noodles. Six months after. Mainly because noodles are carbs and carbs are fat and I couldn't eat noodles anymore. And I missed noodles, because *that Daniel*, he would talk about noodles like Scheherazade weaving threads in the ears of the king. I remember thinking of noodles that day I stood on the scale and seen that I'd done it. There was a thud in my head.

Thud, a ball of dough—rice flour and water and sometimes egg—*thud* it's thrown onto the counter. Supple and craggly and lumpy, *thud*, it's thrown onto the counter and pressed out, flattened, squeezed, pressed until it's a sheet—thin, light, rectangular—*thud*… with knives, with machines, always cut, sliced thin, stretched thin. *Thud.* We are noodles, we begin life as lumps of human starchiness, sliced by the noodle-cutter of life into pretty shapes, acceptable to the human eye and fit for human consumption, *palatable. Thud.* Getting cut, getting sliced, becoming noodled—that hurts. I am the story of lump to linguini.

A shot of pain.

Ow.

'Ant, I did it. 20 kilograms.'

His eyes flicked to the left.

'It was never the weight, Daniel. It was always just you.'

Beat.

Last night, I opened that food blog *that Daniel*, the chubby one, used to write. He was *full*, he saw things. The way we bite our love into our food, cook our love into existence, eat to feel loved, even if it's just me loving me, wishing you loved me. Food fills the gap.

Beat.

I fit into clothes now. I've dropped a few sizes. I've lost 20kg. Lost a small person, really. Lost a small part of me.

A shot of pain.

Got gout instead.

Food, Baby

Kyle Walmsley

An outer suburbs Fasta Pasta.

Amy, 16, enters and takes a seat at her table. The dialogue should be appropriately punctuated by eating, eating action, and food play. She loves drama. Probably the subject at school as well.

AMY The toilets are gross here. Grosser than at school.

Food came. Finally.

You didn't have to wait.

You know what's really random? They say the pasta is faster, but like, faster than what? And how would you even compare something like that. For example, if you had like, a Zinger Burger meal from KFC, and this spaghetti bolognaise what would win in a race? I don't even know. It doesn't even make sense. And I shouldn't really talk about KFC because of... [*she breaks off*]... never mind.

I used to have really bad acne.

From working at KFC.

I was on chips.

Pause.

Just trying to lighten the mood.

Pause.

Are we going to talk about the other night... or... not?

Pause.

Not, I guess.

We need to talk about this, Stephen. I don't know about you but I can't sleep at night. I haven't updated my status for days, and I noticed you didn't respond to my relationship request on Facebook.

She is searching.

Are you wondering why I had to order the gluten free?

I'm a coeliac.

Do you know what that is?

It's a disease.

Like AIDS is a disease.

I can never have wheat. [*Beat.*] I can never have wheat. [*Beat.*] I can never have wheat.

Is that normal, Stephen?

And it's not like anorexia or one of those fake ones, because if I eat wheat my throat could close up and I could die.

So literally, if I eat this and they have forgotten to take all the gluten out... and there is still some gluten left... then I could die... should I risk it... ?

She dangles the spaghetti dramatically above her mouth, eyeballing Stephen all the while. She drops it in, chews and finally swallows. There is a moment where she thinks she could die.

Lucky for you, I'm fine.

Stephen, I just told you that I can't have gluten, and you're looking at your phone. I'm basically disabled, Stephen.

When I told you, you have to come tonight, I said I would pay for your dinner only if you made it a nice night and we could talk about what happened. At the moment, I'm actually really regretting wasting my 2 for 1 voucher on you.

Seriously, why don't you just go?

She cries. She peeks to see if he is checking on her.

God, it's just like at the party.

Bastard!

Pause.

I'm sorry. I'm really emotional at the moment. My hormones are playing up like crazy. You know why... ?

This is embarrassing, but sometimes when I'm really enjoying a meal, I rub my belly back and forwards like there is a baby in it.

Like this, see?

There's not.

Anymore.

No, I'm joking. There never was.

You're just not your usual chatty self tonight, Stephen. So quiet. I can tell you're thinking about it too.

I reckon if I was on one of those shows like Masterchef I'd be really good at the taste challenges. I'm quite good at figuring out what's inside things. What makes things up. That's why I can tell what's going on with you.

Your nose is bleeding.

She watches him as he leaves to go the toilet. She is left not knowing what to do, embarrassed by being alone. She goes through his phone while he's away. Puts its back. Looks around for him. Looks around for longer. This goes on for a long time. She pretends to text on her phone. She sees him. Maybe she listens to her voicemails accidentally on speaker. Maybe she eats his pasta. Maybe she takes the time to stare at everyone else in the restaurant (ie, the audience). He comes back.

What were you doing in there? You were just a really long time. I thought you must have done a runner.

I shouldn't be eating pasta. It makes my eczema get heaps worse. Actually there probably couldn't have been a worse place for me to eat. I just got so excited when you said you'd come. I sometimes just jump into things. I'm really impulsive. But I'm also a perfectionist. Leo. No, Sagittarius. I can't remember. Which is the mermaid one? I think it's Leo. Anyway, it was probably the impulsive part of me that wanted to kiss you at Eloise's party. But I didn't. And it was the perfectionist part of me that didn't. Because you had spew on your shoulder. And your chin. Oh My God, I should not bring that up over food. Oh! Bring it up! [*She pretend vomits. Laughs. Then stops.*] You spewed, remember? I'm so sorry. You're eating. It's so nice here though. I don't often go to the posh places.

I actually came to this exact place on a date with my last boyfriend. And I know you said not to call us boyfriend and... whatever... but relationship or not, I really love the food here. That's why I ate so much. So fancy. Like how they come and check on you, and when the guy pulled out the chair I was like—what? Nah, it's all good.

Can I just say, sorry for bringing up Matthew. Just then in that story. I shouldn't really mention him on a date with somebody else… if this is a date… well, I know it's a date, but… you're way hotter than he was. I reckon he's richer than you though, and that's not me having a go at you, he just went to the private school that Cate Blanchette's kids go to, and his Mum died from some sort of weird armpit cancer or something, and he got heaps of money. She was an interior decorator. She'd love this place if she was here tonight. And alive. Obviously. Sorry.

They're probably going to come and take our plates in a minute. Once you're finished.

It's only been a moment.

I'm sorry. This silence is killing me. I just can't play your mind games, Stephen. I have to say something, and I know you've got stuff to say too, but can I just speak for once? I've just got be brave and tell you.

She stands.

Do we want dessert? That's not the thing. I just thought now I'm standing, they're probably going to come over and ask if we want dessert. Anyway, just think about that, so we can just say if he comes over.

I know we're both thinking about the other night, and to save the awkwardness, and to make sure I didn't just word vomit all over you—sorry—I prepared a range of possible questions you might ask, and then a corresponding set of possible answers to those possible questions. I'm just going to read them to you now.

She takes out a piece of paper and reads from it.

Question One: Amy, will you marry me?

Answer: Stephen, your heart knows no limits. Yes, I will.

Question Two: Amy, Will you break up with me?

Answer: Stephen, No.

So, that's good, I feel better now that's out of the way. Cleared the air a little bit. And I guess now we can just enjoy ourselves. Order dessert. I might get another coke. If this waiter ever comes over.

She looks around trying to catch a waiter's eye. She tries and tries again.

She has no luck.

Probably just get it without rum. Like yours at the party? When you were having rum and coke? Not surprising you don't remember.

That night... at the party... I think you were *really* sexy the night of the party, I did... I do... even with the spew on your shoulder. And on your chin.

You were sitting on the couch and I just

Kissed you.

I'm sorry.

That's *rape*. I know.

I said I didn't but I did. Oh, this is why it sucks to be a Leo.

But I did it.

I feel sick still thinking about it.

She does another fake spew. It's an attempt at relieving the tension. She laughs.

Sorry.

I didn't really even know that much about what I was doing. But I've watched pornos. Not normally. But just in case something like this came up. Just so I had an idea of what to do.

[*Fishing*] You probably hate me now.

She keeps an eye on him. Carefully planning her next move.

Especially because of... never mind...

Beat. She is crying.

Sometimes I feel like I try too hard. To impress people. Or like, like, being relaxed people will find me boring, or not people but you, you will find me boring, boys will find me boring, and I'm not that smart so I don't really want to be a smart girl, and I actually really like people, and I like it when other people are interesting, and I only say that because when I find other people boring I hate them. Which is why I think I hate myself.

Big sobs. Silence.

Please say something, Stephen.

Suddenly, she stops crying.

For God's sake, what's it going to take? I just gave the performance of my lifetime, and I may as well be talking to the flippen spaghetti! I know you still like me, because otherwise why would you still be here finishing off the meal I bought for you!

Maybe I'm just over thinking things. I don't really get why I was having this weird feeling you were going to break up with me tonight. And if you are feeling that, then what I would say is... *don't*. Okay?

See, it's kind of like this meal.

[*Scarily intense*] See how it's finished and you might think, oh well. It's over. And it sort of is. But, it sort of isn't, too. See? There's a few little crumbs scattered around the edges of the plate still... [*She slaps his hand away or moves the plate out of reach.*] No. Don't try eating them. And, you have to remember that in a few hours you'll be hungry again. It never ends. So although it may feel like we need to stop eating. That it's ending. It doesn't. We don't. Otherwise we'll die. And no one wants to die, right? Because the food lives on even after the meal is finished. In our mouths and in our tummies. Then you get the satisfaction of licking your lips,

Feeling your food baby...

Which is a real baby...

I'm pregnant.

[*To the waiter*] We'll have dessert please.

George

Keir Wilkins

A large metal drum sits centre stage, acting as a crude campfire. Atop it, a fully decorated Christmas tree is being licked by the flames.

LJ, malnourished and dirty, takes a seat on a crate next to the fire, mustering as much composure as possible, despite being visibly shaken.

LJ I want to tell you… all of you… I hope maybe if I do, you'll understand. 'Cause I know what people have been saying. But… I just… I just… I feel like what you're about to do… we're going down a path… you get that we can't go back after this? I just… I know if I tell you about George… Then you could decide. Please?

Can I tell you about George?

Silence. LJ takes this as permission to proceed.

We're living on an abandoned property. They have animals, you know? The petrol's run out. Nothing grows. Just dead earth. Me, Mum, Dad and George, just waiting I guess. Waiting to be told what to do. We band together with the others left in Augusta. People are getting desperate… that's when we start to slip I think. To detach.

At first everyone loves George. I guess my parents are happy to have him around 'cause it keeps me happy. But then food starts running out and people grow more and more desperate. They start resenting me feeding him. *'He's a dog, and right now, we take priority.'* I try to tell them, make them understand. He's my best friend. He's more than that.

LJ snaps out of the memory, returning to the present.

I know this might not mean much… to you. Not now. But everyone has a George. Remember? Remember who your George was. You know?

I'm at the footy oval with George when we find out. He's been acting weird all morning. Like he's depressed or something. Then he wanders off and I can't find him anywhere.

I'd had him since my 8th birthday you know? Dad named him. George. After George Orwell. His favourite writer. Always used to say lines from his books. At the dinner table, he'd reach over and take the last piece of steak, shepherds pie, whatever. He'd say, 'All animals are created equal. But some animals are more equal than others.'

That day, I can't find George. That's when it comes on the radio. People have the radio on, listening to the top 100.

It's weird, thinking about it now, don't you think? No one really knew what an extinction level event was. Just made me think of the dinosaurs you know? Like there'd be a big massive bang and then lights out. Not this. This waiting. Not knowing.

George came home later that night but I still believe he knew. Before we did. People say, *'that's just instincts'*. But it's more than that.

LJ becomes emotional, but pulls it together, annoyed at the show of weakness.

I'm sorry, I don't mean to… I'm not trying to get all… But you have to… it's what I want to tell you. I'm not just trying to save myself. But I've had so much time to think about this. About where we're headed. About how it was. You know, I think back and I feel sick. All the times I'd load up my plate, get full after a few bites and ditch the rest. But I hate the blamers. Spending all day trying to work out whose fault it is? We all did this. All of us together.

Silence.

Dad mentions it first. He's nervous. We'd lost Mum by then. I guess people told him to do it. He says *'we haven't eaten in 60 hours. I don't know where the next food is gonna come from.'* Like I don't know that. Like my stomach isn't twisted in knots I'm so hungry. He tells me that some of the others in the camp have brought up… maybe… the possibility… that George, *I mean he's an old dog, and besides, Indians and the Chinese eat dog…*

George is smart. That's what I say first. My first argument. He knows what's going on. He senses things. Dad keeps telling me to be logical. Rational. But how can I be? In the end, the best I can come up with is that I love George. You don't eat your loved ones. I mean… Mum gave him to me. He has a personality and memories and fears. He likes some foods and not others. He likes some people and not others. He dreams! *'It's comparative intelligence. Compared to us… he's a dog. He's flesh. And we need to survive.'*

LJ remembers something. Something uncomfortable. It's a struggle to find the words…

One of the people staying with us has a daughter, Angie. She's like… mentally disabled, you know? And I remember her Mum once told me that a doctor said that Angie had the brain of a three year old… or a really smart dog. *'Would you eat her Dad? Would you eat Angie?'* *'That's not the same and you know it,'* he says. And I think he's right, but I'm not sure I know why. *'All animals are created equal, but some are more equal than others.'*

LJ can sense the discomfort and grows desperate to finish what was started.

Please! Wait! I know it's not making sense right now. None of this makes any sense. But that's when it started. It started with George. When we slipped. When we… I wanted to tell you…

A long silence. The next words take some strength.

Eating George was weird. I think my brain left my body. It was like everything and nothing. It was like… falling out of love… or something. Something beautiful… suddenly you can only see it for what it is. Pores, sweat and hot breath. Just flesh. Yeah, that feeling of everything and nothing. That's what it was like eating George.

It was the most I'd eaten in ages. But I didn't feel full. I felt empty.

I know Dad felt the same. I think maybe that's what tipped him over the edge. George tore him open and once his soul was gone… his body just gave up.

See, that's why I wanted to tell you. Because I know people have been talking. I know that I'm next. And maybe I deserve it. I mean what argument can *I* make that I couldn't have made for George? I have a personality and memories and fears. I like some foods and not others. I like some people and not others. I dream.

Or maybe I'm just flesh.

All I know is… I won't nourish you. And I won't fill you.

And that's what I wanted to tell you.

LJ's head lowers mercifully, then rises, eyes full of fear.

Please.

Blackout.

The Language of Love
Kim Ho

Charlie sits nervously in his chair, poring over a paper on his desk. He's doing a French exam, and is on to the last question. Even though he's speaking, no one around him seems to hear.

Charlie 'Writing Task B. Describe your best friend.' Oh God, not this again. 'What qualities do you admire in them? What are their favourite activities?' Blah, blah… hobbies… letter? 'Write your response as a letter to your friend, in French.'

Well, shit.

This exam was going so well until now. I never know what to write for these questions. I mean, do I make up a best friend, or do I talk about Sam? I can do all the grammar exercises, it's just expressing myself that's the hard part. I'm never going to be fluent. I mean, that was aim: speak French like a Frenchman. Well actually, the aim was to pick up chicks by sounding like a Frenchman. Hasn't really worked out yet.

French is not like maths, where there's only one right answer. Like, even if you learn all the words in the dictionary it doesn't mean you can speak the language. A whole group of guys went over to France on exchange, although apparently it was just this non-stop root-fest with all the naughty angels.

Is that it? Pillow talking your way to fluency?

And there are all these traps in the language. Like the word 'baiser' means 'to kiss' and 'to fuck,' and the only difference is context. I mean, who would do that? I can imagine some sad French dude thinking that up just to make it hard for… for people like me.

Sam and I do everything together. Eat. Piss. Muck about in French. We steal all the whiteboard markers when our teacher's late to class. We would sit together too, but Monsieur Edgerton likes the seating alphabetical, so Sam's been put right in front of me. I've been staring at the back of his head now for three and a half terms, and we're very well acquainted.

It does get a bit annoying, his head blocking my view all the time. 'Specially on Friday afternoons when we get to watch a film—

apparently all French movies are called films. Sometimes I tap him on the shoulder and when he turns round I flick a rubber band at him. Although I haven't really been doing that recently. His parents are going through a divorce and he comes to school all like morose, you know? Like, he smiles and all that, but you can see in his eyes that he's hurting pretty bad inside. In class, he's stopped turning round. He just sits, hunched over. Fidgets with his pencil case.

It's been a shit year for him. Wanted to get into like the firsts Basketball, but they moved him down instead cos he's become sort of 'distant'. When I asked him about it he just jabbed me in the arm with his locker key.

I don't have such grand aspirations. I um... I wanted to be head librarian. I got it, cos I can wrap books better than the teachers can. That, and I don't steal the sex ed. books. *The Karma Sutra, a Graphic Guide. Avoiding Gonorrhea for Dummies.*

Gonorrhea.

Sounds like a name from Shakespeare, doesn't it? Cordelia, Regan, Gonorrhea. I got a badge, too. For Library. It's gold, and shiny I'm in love with Sam.

I'm in love with my best friend.

Dunno how it happened... just somewhere along the line of listening to his secrets and seeing how hurt he was I realised how much I care. I want to hold him, tell him everything's gonna be okay.

The fuck is happening to me?

Like, my heart beats faster when he's around, and I can't think about anybody else. I don't need that, 'specially not in a French exam. But I can't help it. I can't control it. I try and do my homework but my mind keeps wandering, and I'm sitting in French over and over again. Mr. Edgerton's playing a film, but I'm watching Sam. I see the outline of his face silhouetted against the projector screen, and I want to see his eyes, touch his cheek, press my lips to his... and it scares me shitless.

I Googled, 'How to tell a guy you like him,' but all the results were about how much makeup to use. I wouldn't dare say a word to him. I mean, how would I even start? 'Hi Sam, hope your parents haven't murdered each other yet. I'm gay. Are you gay? Do you want to cuddle, or something?'

I'm afraid.

Afraid that I'll ask him to kiss me… and he'll get the wrong idea. Think I'm a creep, y'know? It's not cos he's a boy, he just happens to be one. And I can't figure out whether that makes it wrong or special.

I know what my mates'd say. One time, we went down to the beach, just laughing and mucking about. But, y'know, 'Tanning is skin cells in trauma,' so I offered to put sunscreen on Sam's back. He just smiled, said it was fine, but the other guys howled me down. Didn't let me forget how gay I'd acted. 'Charlie's a poofter!' But I don't want to forget. I don't want to forget Sam running back from the surf, shaking the water out of his hair. Big grin on his face.

I want what's best for him; I really do. But I also want him for myself. I want to be what's best for him.

Am I just being selfish? He's my best friend, and he means more to me than any Band 6 exam mark. Maybe the best thing to do is just keep this inside and squash it. But I don't want to betray him. He trusts me. He opens up to me.

Shouldn't I do the same?

'Charlie's a poofter.' You always hear people saying it's 'weird' and 'just not normal'. But isn't that the point of love? To transcend normalness and become something special? Maybe the French would even back me. I mean, *amour* is a masculine noun.

I have to take the plunge. Open my mouth and tell that beautiful boy how I feel.

A letter.

Mon cher Samuel.

Je t'aime.

Hunger

Brooke Robinson

Sam, 17
A restaurant kitchen.

SAM:

Gas flames
dishes stacked
added to
more orders!
In my uniform so bleached I could disappear
I'm still chopping the red stuff
TABLE 5 COMING
concentrate
vertical strokes
(just like you)
my knife slips
shit
splats on the floor
I'LL CLEAN IT UP
I bend down
sop up the red
no room to move
in single file
my shoes touching with those of the next kitchen hand
I level back up to the stove
my head catches a saucepan handle as I rise
oh god
not again

tossed over
the pan soars
liquids slop
the whole kitchen quakes with fear
NEXT ORDER
IT'S COMING
spoon to lips
taste
tongue around
latch onto that layer of
nothing
I… can't
nothing left
keep stirring
IT'S COMING
you grunt
spittle in the air
no time
stir
what
what's that
a red drop crawls along the inside of the saucepan
IT'S COMING I SAID
the red inches down
before I can act
hits the surface of the liquid
and spreads
blood
oh shit!
flip over my hands
burns

scabs
thick skin
the usual
eyes off the stove
you hit me across the back of the head
My neck snaps
a cut
there
a hole in my left arm
you grab the saucepan handle
rip it off the heat
dip the spoon in
push it to your ruddy face
no
no
no
what are you doing
you can't
I NEED FIVE MORE MINUTES
you shake your head
please
you're not listening
no
you can't take that out
IT'S NOT READY
I...
you turn to face me
YOU WHAT
I suck in some air
nothing
It's fine

get it out there

shit

food lapped onto two plates

I hold my breath

look up through the skylight in the kitchen ceiling

just for a second

We're not supposed to do this but you're not looking so I stick my head round into the dining room

shoulders hunched my four fingers grip the wall

I'd forgotten how white the room is all walls, clean tablecloths and crockery

the smell of pale roses

I watch the waiter glide over to two women at the corner table

I look down at the cut in my arm and a new droplet of blood pauses between skin and floor

the jaws of the women slacken and slide for what feels like infinity

as a black crust forms over my lungs and I can't keep going on like this

I just need to breathe

and

then

she smiles

the older of the two women smiles

she digs her spoon back in deep

masticates

swallows

and smiles again

my lungs relax

it's fine

you didn't see the blood

they didn't taste the blood

kitchen sounds burrow inside

white noise of

silver on silver

and the slow peel and burn of the lacquer on the bottom of
saucepans

standing next to me

your skin cooled to a rare soft pink

nice

you say

good work

they told the waiter

the women

compliments to the chef

they want more

table 7 and 8 overheard and want to order it too

Three minutes, you bark

Okay

Keep stirring

oh god

that means

it was

the blood

no

TWO MINUTES KID

no

no

I can't

that

I

ONE MINUTE

no

shit

Hunger

do something
recipe
red stuff
heat
green stuff
spoon in
taste
it's empty
it's nothing
I
can't do this
I
can't
do
it
you're
standing close
you're smiling but your hand is raised and it sweeps through the air,
I flinch instinctively as your hand swoops and stops to a
sudden
pat
on my shoulder
the three layers of fabric between your palm and my shoulder
unravel to thread and I can feel your skin on mine
it's my blood
my insides you want and you don't even know it
I trace my index finger around the cut on my arm
the edges bend
release
one
two

three drops into the saucepan
stir it in clockwise
that's it
no more
that's all I've got to give
IT'S READY
you snatch at the saucepan and the plates disappear
MORE KID MORE
your lips apart
teeth jutting out
but I'm not scared
the others
muted
the kitchen
silent
I grab extra saucepans
fire up all the hot plates
have four going at once
nobody's looking
paw at my arm wound
do ten drops in each saucepan
spoon slashing a figure eight between pans one, two, three, four
I'm losing a lot of blood now
hold on to the side of the bench
my weight skids
away from me
catch sight of my arm
the outline erased
bunch up my uniform and see the arm flesh is... faded
MORE ORDERS KID YOU'RE DOING GREAT
more blood leaks and drips to the floor

a sticky pool underfoot
but my shoes
not in the mess
they're
hovering
slightly
in the air
ankle height
resting on an invisible shelf
COME ON I'M WAITING
air escapes my lungs
Snap!
I'm heavy again
my feet drop to the floor
back to work
Plates lined up
gleaming and perfect
catch your eye thrown back at me in the surface of a pan
the way you're looking
at me
you're happy
you're actually proud
new saucepans
new spoons
even before I start stirring
hang my arm over the pan
a transparent limb now
feather-light
pour in a cup of my secret ingredient
MORE
circling above my head

stirring
all the way up to the skylight in the ceiling
I cover the pots
let them simmer
I want to see their faces!
lean my head out the back door to the outdoor seating area
An elderly couple
eating my dish
deep smiles across both faces
I smile back and wave
but my arm
doesn't actually raise
a shadow moves but the flesh and bone
I can't budge
can't control it
I spy the next table of diners
nodding and chewing
a helium balloon reads: HAPPY BIRTHDAY
it hovers near a gas heater by a little girl
WHERE'S THE FOOD BOY
stirring again, both pans
I dish it out
new batch
simmering
the blood's still dripping from my cut
but the red has gone out of it
DONE!
out of the back window my eye catches the little girl's birthday
balloon
it bobs up and down but always comes to still lower than it began
some helium has leaked out

Hunger

I feel
taller
myself
lighter and
free
as if the helium has leeched through to me
and YES
I look down
my feet
not touching the ground
I kick my legs
reach up and rise another few centimeters
the balloon drops again
as if a counter weight
instantly I rise another few centimeters
the balloon lowers further towards the ground I rise upward,
keeping the balance of things
you leave the kitchen for the outside dining area
I call out, point down with my toes but you can't hear me or see me
I'm floating too high up now far beyond your reach
There's a grey smudge in your hand
a fork
you approach the table with the little girl but your knee buckles and
you trip
lose your balance for a moment and the fork runs straight into the
balloon
POP!
it sinks
dead
I SOAR
alive
I can't stop it now

I'm
higher
under my skin I feel my blood heated to boiling point
but a gentle boil from liquid to vapor and now it's free

AUTHOR BIOGRAPHIES

Jory Anast (*Pip Nat Georgie*) is in her third and final year of a BFA degree at QUT, majoring in Creative and Professional Writing, and Film, Television and Screen. She is a poet, a playwright, a screenwriter and a short story enthusiast.

Jake Brain (*Tell Me*) graduated from the University of Technology Sydney in 2012 with a Bachelor of Communication, majoring in Writing and Cultural Studies. He attended the Metroscreen ArtStart Screenwriters program in 2011 and the Fresh Ink National Studio in 2013.

Sophie Hardcastle (*Sweet Sour*) studied Fine Arts at Sydney College of the Arts after being fast-tracked into the course by International artist Lindy Lee. Recently, however, she suspended her studies to focus on her writing. She has since finished her second novel, having already written an 80,000-word novel at the age of fifteen and an 8000 word short story at the age of seventeen. Although having no experience as a playwright, Sophie won a Mosman Literary Prize in 2010 for her prose and a NSW Premier's award for All Round Excellence in 2011. Sophie's work has also been published in *Surfing World* magazine.

Tasnim Hossain (*Sweet in the Savoury*) is a performance poet and playwright from Canberra. She is completing her Bachelor of Arts (International Relations), majoring in International Communications, at ANU and has worked in drama outreach programs run by the university, as well as poetry slam workshops funded by Arts ACT. She is passionate about working with young people and is one of Canberra Youth Theatre's Associate Playwrights for 2013. She has performed around Canberra at poetry slams as well as at Multifringe 9.2.13, the fringe component of the National Multicultural Festival in 2013, and at the You Are Here festival in 2011. She is interested in writing about what home and belonging means for people of different generations, cultures and gender identities, as well as the intersections where people from different backgrounds meet. She is currently working on a short play for Canberra Youth Theatre's season of staged readings.

Julian Larnach (*Something I Prepared Earlier*) is a Sydney-based playwright. This year Julian is Affiliate Writer at Griffin Theatre Company and is undertaking an Australian Council for the Arts JUMP Mentorship with Melbourne Theatre Company's literary manager, Chris Mead. He was also selected for Playwriting Australia's National

Script Workshop and was short listed for PWA's Re-Gen Seed Commission. He has recently completed creative developments for new works with the Australian Theatre for Young People, Darwin's National Youth Week Festival, NIDA Independent and Griffin Theatre. Julian holds a Bachelor of Arts (Government and International Relations, 2011) and a Graduate Diploma in Dramatic Art (Playwriting, 2012) from the National Institute of Dramatic Art.

Zac Linford (*Dig In Dean*) is a Geelong based writer currently enrolled in his third year of Professional and Creative Writing at Deakin University. He is a member of the Arts Advisory Panel and a board member for Courthouse Arts, where he contributes to ongoing art events, collaborations and involving the youth in Geelong and the Bellarine. Zac also participated in the Fresh Ink 4×4 playwright mentorship at Courthouse ARTS (Geelong). Influenced by misheard sayings and half-hearted conversations, Zac's style and interests stretch to all forms of creative communication. At present he is working on several scripts and collaborations with fellow writers and directors in the industry.

Felicity Pickering (*Facon*) is a playwright and writer. She has been published in the *Stonesthrow Review* (State University of New York, New Paltz Writing Anthology), *Picture 1000 Words* (a photo-literary collaboration), *The Evening Lands* (2013 UTS Writers' Anthology) and other publications. In 2012, Felicity was short listed for the Monash Undergraduate Prize for Creative Writing, leading her to be published in a Penguin Special. Felicity has a passion for dramatic writing and spoken word. She has had two plays produced: *The Banquet* (2011) and *Neighbours* (2012). In 2012, she performed in Freshly Squeezed as part of performance troupe: 'The Cabana Bay Club Dancers', which led to a residency at the Joan Sutherland Theatre. Felicity has volunteered at Under The Radar, an experimental theatre festival in New York, and been a Dramaturgy Intern for PlayWriting Australia. In 2013, Felicity completed a honours thesis exploring the performance identity in the slam poetry movement, with a focus on the Australasia scene. She writes reviews on her blog: http://fliction.wordpress.com/

Emily Sheehan (*Eating Sunshine*) is an actor, writer and theatre maker. She has an Advanced Diploma of Arts (Stage & Screen Acting) from the Actors College of Theatre & Television, and a Bachelor of Arts (Theatre Studies) from the University of New England. In 2013 she received a scholarship to study Improvisation and Comedy Writing at the Second

City Training Centre in Chicago. Emily's stage credits include *Dance Hall Days* (Q Theatre Company), *This is Baby Doll* (Factotum Theatre), *And The Winner Is* (Perform Educational Musicals). Television credits include *Deadly Women* (Beyond Productions) and *Dark Minds* (Beyond Productions). Emily was nominated for Best Actress at the Australian Webstream Awards for her role in *The Drive Web Series*.

Joel Tan (*That Daniel*) is a playwright and performer. He read English Literature at the National University of Singapore where he also studied playwriting with Huzir Sulaiman. He made his professional playwriting debut in 2011 with W!ld Rice's production of *Family Outing*, which premiered as part of the Man-Singapore Theatre Festival. Since then, he has been active as a playwright, director and dramaturg in Singapore's young-people's theatre scene, mounting full productions of his most recent plays, *Postgrads* (Takeoff Productions) and *People* (USP Productions). Joel works closely with other young theatre makers to create theatre that is challenging, beautiful and relevant. To this end, he has mentored young participants of Buds Youth Theatre in playwriting and is a core member of Takeoff Productions, a small independent theatre company dedicated to commissioning new writing by emerging playwrights. Joel's attendance at the Studio has been made possible through the support of the National Arts Council (Singapore) and in collaboration with Checkpoint Theatre (Singapore), where Joel is an Associate Artist.

Kyle Walmsley (*Food, Baby*) is a graduate of the acting program at the University of Southern Queensland, Toowoomba. Kyle has performed for Polyglot Theatre Company, Queensland Arts Council, Darwin Theatre Company, Here Today Theatre Company and Corrugated Iron Youth Arts. Kyle was a national finalist in the Melbourne International Comedy Festival's Raw Comedy Competition in 2012. Kyle has written shows for Queensland Arts Council, and Corrugated Iron Youth Arts, and is also an emerging arts writer currently undergoing a mentorship with Next Wave Festival and writing for his own blog: imverytiredandcranky.blogspot.com.

Keir Wilkins (*George*) is a writer from Perth, Western Australia. After completing his BA in Film and Performance Studies, he went on to gain a Graduate Diploma in Screenwriting from AFTRS in Sydney. His short films have been recognised in both national and international film festivals and he was recently named Best Young Australian Filmmaker at the Shorts Film Festival and as Young WA Filmmaker of the Year at the WA Screen Awards. In 2012, Keir worked as a script attachment on the Matchbox Pictures telemovie *Underground, the Julian Assange Story* and as a creative writer on Arena Media's feature film *The Turning*. He is currently in development on his half hour television comedy series *Miseducation*, with Hatch Entertainment and *Boy Jam*, with ScreenWest. For the stage, Keir wrote *Fighting Words* for Powerhouse Youth Theatre.

Kim Ho (*The Language of Love*) was born and raised in Sydney. Throughout his schooling, he was heavily involved in music and drama, performing in plays such as *The Popular Mechanicals*, Louis Nowra's *Cosi* and Monty Python's *Spamalot*. He is also involved in community theatre, and has played an ungodly number of animals: springboks, foxes, crabs, and horses. And a tumbleweed. Kim enjoys storytelling in all its forms, and has made several short films for Tropfest Jr. However, he really began focusing on dramatic writing in 2012. The success of *Transcendence* in The Voices Project's Love Bytes competition led to a mentorship with Tommy Murphy. Together, they developed his monologue *The Language of Love*, which enjoyed worldwide exposure. In 2013, he was a recipient of the Besen Family Artist Programme, Writer's Development at Malthouse Theatre. Kim is currently developing a deliciously wicked black comedy, and devours every play he finds.

Brooke Robinson (*Hunger*) was a member of the 2011 Australian Theatre for Young People's Fresh Ink Writers ensemble. There she wrote *Hunger*, performed as part of the stage show The Voices Project 2012: The One Sure Thing season, directed by Tanya Goldberg. *Hunger* is published by Currency Press and has been made into a short film, directed by Stephen McCallum (read the interview with Stephen on page 19 of this book). *Dangerous Lenses* was produced by The Impending Room at Old 505 Theatre in Sydney in October 2012 and traveled to the Hub Station in Melbourne in September 2013 where it was highly commended in the Melbourne Fringe Festival Writing Award category. *Teeth* was commissioned for Tamarama Rock Surfers' 2013 Bondi Feast Festival. Brooke holds degrees in Literature and Creative Writing from the University of Sydney and the University of Technology Sydney.

.